LOVE
INCORPORATED

GADFLY

First Published 2020
Gadfly

© 2020 Martyn Clark

ISBN 978-1-9162497-0-7 Paperback
ISBN 978-1-9162497-1-4 Hardcover

British Library Cataloguing in Publication Data. A CIP catalogue record for this book is available from the British Library. Martyn Clark has asserted his right to be identified as the Author of this work in accordance with the Copyright, Designs and Patents Act 1988. All rights reserved. No part of this publication may be reproduced without prior permission. Typeset in Adobe Caslon Pro 11pt. This book was written and produced during a period of twenty four continuous days, including typesetting design, editing, indexing, and artwork. Gadfly is an imprint of Gadfly Editions, Kemp House, 152-160 City Road, London EC1V 2NX.

www.gadflygroup.com

*In memory of
Georges*

Contents

Prologue	13
Learning to walk again	19
Everyday happenings	55
Into the psyche	103
Gadfly principles	123
Core conditions	139
Leading systemic change	163
The future of business	191
Postlude	199

Love
Incorporated

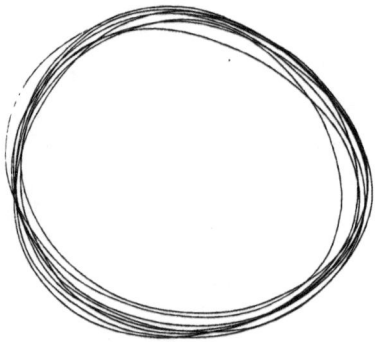

Prologue

I am the King Rat. I don't quite know how I got the part. Neil said that we should audition, and I just went along with him. Miss Keene, the teacher with the scary glasses, chose *me*. It's 1979. I'm eight. I am sitting on top of my classmates' shoulders, sheets of blue silk billowing around me. The Pied Piper isn't far behind, but I have to sing this song before I drown, and people will clap a lot for me. I have my whole life in front of me. It's going to be *amazing*. I'm going to do lots of singing and dancing, and be a politician, and have lots of girlfriends, make lots of money, have a big house, get married, and live a perfect life. I will have a business, work with important people, and fly in *Concorde* a lot. But I'm not sure how people choose just one person to live with. This book is the story of how I learned that being me is probably the best, and scariest, thing I could ever hope to achieve.

I just spoke with Richard O'Connor, Global Head of Investor Relations at HSBC. Richard was one of my first clients in the finance sector, sixteen years ago, before the crash, before my injury, before we all knew about global warming. Twenty four years after being the King Rat. Over the years, Richard and I have had many herbal teas while talking about the state of the world, the future of capitalism, and my bizarre interests in studying anarchic leadership and eastern philosophy. He has me pinned as a 'green advocate'. It's not how I would describe myself; I just like picking systems apart, solving the toughest problems that I can find, and helping people to face whatever underlying reality is uncovered.

We are in a time when we need to construct organisations very differently. The way we do business is having a shockingly negative impact on the environment, on mental health, on our future as a species. It doesn't take much research to see that in every way, our current system is under stress. Every problem I see has this common root, and I can no longer ignore these systemic issues. Here at Gadfly, we have a dream: we want to change the way business is done, so that together, we can change the world. We want to offer our experience of leading large scale change, so that we can transform institutions, businesses, supply chains, education, transport systems, philosophies. We want to support leaders to rise to the challenge of facing, head-on, the biggest problems that mankind has ever faced. We want to do what we can to help. This book is a step.

I also talked to Sezgin Kaya today, a Director at Deloitte, who I've known since working together in 2012. I was in the middle of finalising the book cover, having received feedback on the initial design and content from designers, brand consultants, a marketing and insight director, human resources and leadership consultants, a member of the judiciary, and many clients, male and female, young and old, from across eleven countries. Unsurprisingly, there wasn't a consistent theme to the feedback. Some found my writing self-indulgent, some found it inspiring. Some found it hard to read. Others found it easy. Some have decided that I'm so narcissistic that they want nothing to do with me, and others found it so personally touching that they want to meet for coffee. We've nudged the language, taking the feedback into account, rewritten a few sections, and redesigned the cover to more powerfully frame the message. We now need to stop fiddling, and publish it, aware that it's imperfect and has some inconsistencies.

Sez reminded me that the future of business is this kind of diversity. Diverse opinions, perspectives, voices, narratives, and finding a way to tolerate the conflicts, misunderstandings, and paradoxical multiple truths that we encounter in any situation. He suggested that we should find a way to frame my writing with a foreword, or multiple forewords, written by people who know me well, so that people who don't know me don't misunderstand my intention. It might help people understand the importance of relationship—with people, place, and self—to the future of business. Sez is right: a diversity of voices is probably the only way to capture the essence of what I've tried to achieve through writing. He knows me well. So please bear in mind, as you read, that we would love to add your voice to the conversation in some way.

This book is an attempt to weave together concepts from systems analysis, large scale organisational change, coaching, creativity, personal stories, philosophy, and spiritual disciplines. I'm offering some of my experiences as metaphors: they can perhaps help you to discover something about yourself and your life. We want this book to be a journey for you. We're aware that we probably won't quite achieve the level of elegance that we would like to, and that the journey may not be as smooth as we would like it to be. Some sections may work well for you, and others may not. Some you may need to revisit, as I may not have explained different concepts well enough, or you may need more of the story to be able to understand it fully. I apologise in advance if you feel lost, but sometimes I felt lost while writing, and we chose to not remove that from the story, as it's all part of the journey. I've tried to keep the journey as simple as possible, and as a result, it has ended up being paradoxically quite complex.

This isn't a conventional business book. It started as scribbled notes taken between client sessions with corporate executives, and drawings made during coaching and consultancy work, to explain complex concepts to leaders. I studied physics, systems analysis, music, and surgical sciences at postgraduate level, and have completed lots of training in leadership, psychotherapy, executive coaching, and martial arts. As a result, my way of viewing the world is rather unique. I tend to start with basic principles, holding conventions lightly, and beginning with a white piece of paper. I work with emotion, analysis, systemic thinking, and creativity. It's just how I personally approach any problem.

This isn't a philosophy book. This isn't a business book. It's not an innovation book, or a Zen book, a therapy book, travelogue, or a book of personal stories and experiences. It's all of those things, woven together. As a result, at times it is a little disjointed, confusing, and awkward. We've tried our best to tie it together in ways that might be useful, or might touch you in some way. My intent in writing has been to leave you with a sense of your unique perspective being valuable, and to leave you with slightly different expectations of the world, the organisations that you're part of, and of yourself as a contributor to society. Our hope is that as you read, you might see your role as a leader more clearly, and be more aware of the importance of the 'soft' side of business.

You're likely to be irritated at some points, as the story jumps around quite a bit. It's all part of the journey of this book. Please give it a chance, and just let your irritation be. It's the intended effect. There's a reason our company is called Gadfly, after all. By Socrates' definition, a gadfly is an individual who challenges the status quo, a horse fly, a small, persistent irritant that provokes change.

By the end of the book, we hope you will want to leaf through it again. You might understand some things better on a second pass. Think of it as a puzzle that gradually unfolds, that you can approach in any direction you want, starting anywhere, but which won't become clear until you've seen how all of the pieces fit together.

> *All we can ever aspire to is already inside us:*
> *our task in life is to reveal it, and to accept it.*

Learning to walk again

I'm sitting in a forest in southern Switzerland, a few kilometres from the Italian border. My teenage son is spending the day with a surgeon in Lugano hospital, observing intestinal surgery. I decided to stay in the area for the day, to walk in the mountains. I am exploring, off the beaten track, a group of mountains called *Denti Della Vecchia*: Old Woman's Teeth. I'm sitting on a marker from 1928 that has been used for generations to map the terrain and provide a solid reference point from which measurements can be taken. I grew up in Switzerland, in a little french-speaking village called Court, in the *Jura-Bernois*. I was the son of the minister in the local church, a congregation full of watchmakers, farmers, teachers and nurses. When I wasn't at school, in church, milking cows on the local farm, or hanging out in watch-making factories, I spent days wandering in the mountains, learning about forests, animals, and the ways of the wild. I learned how to read the weather from the direction of the winds, how to find *morille* and *cep* mushrooms, how to tread lightly in the natural world, and respect its awesome power. I learned to predict snow falls, to find my own path through the woods, and how to be safe on even the roughest, most dangerous, terrain. I learned how to chase *chamoix*, the wild mountain goat-antelopes that make crazy leaps into the unknown over the edge of cliffs, landing on the smallest ledges. I even learned to yodel. In short, I was a young mountain man.

Over the years, I moved a lot. Ireland, England, Italy, America, eventually settling in Scotland, where I somehow lost my connection to the mountains, and to wildness. I studied Physics, singing, and surgery, married, found work, got a mortgage, had kids, and eventually found my way into board-level consultancy. I worked my way up the consultancy 'ladder', and at the height of the madness that was the 2007 bubble, I was working with leaders across the banking industry, a trusted advisor on communication, innovation, and large scale change. I did a lot of work at senior levels in the Royal Bank of Scotland Group, at the peak of their 'success', supporting leaders to see beyond their fixed frames of reference, encouraging thinking that was less black and white, and coaching them to become better communicators and more rounded leaders.

I wasn't prepared for what happened next. In 2011, having survived the Crash and the shockwaves that hit the banking sector, I took some time out to research new styles of leadership. After moving to a new home, I suddenly developed serious issues with my lungs. My whole life, I had mild asthma: nothing that a quick burst of inhaler couldn't fix. This was different. My high-flying life was brought to a standstill. Within weeks, I could barely walk the 100 metres to the local park, never mind the hours of walking that I did every day while working with clients in cities around the world. Overnight, I went from exercising for 20-30 hours a week to barely moving. By spring of 2012, I had a chest infection, was on oral steroids, and was mostly sitting, watching the spring leaves unfurl, knowing I had to wait for my body to heal.

> *Pain is an opportunity for growth
> and learning, but only if we embrace it,
> and don't take it personally.*

I managed to keep going for almost a year, doing some large pieces of work, and hiring a personal assistant to try to take some of the load from me. By 2013, though, I couldn't continue any more. I was exhausted, depressed, and struggling to find the motivation for anything in life. Struggling to breathe is one of the toughest challenges I have ever faced. The following 6 years involved repeated lung infections, pneumonia, exhaustive (and exhausting) tests of my lungs, hideous rounds of medication, including more oral steroids, followed by bone scans, to ensure that my bones weren't being harmed by the drugs. It wasn't until three years later that my pulmonologist worked out that the cause was penetrating damp and mould in the walls of the house I was living in. By that stage, my work had completely ground to a halt. I had no insurance to cover such an incident. It felt like my life was over.

By then, we also had major building work going on, with every room in the house being affected by mould, damp, and hidden contamination, and legal action to recoup the losses.

We moved as soon as we could, and my symptoms immediately started to resolve, but it has taken a few years for my lungs to recover, and they're still not quite right. So, I've spent two and a half years taking walks in the mountains on the Swiss-Italian border, very gradually rebuilding my strength and lung capacity. I've been off all asthma medication for a month now, and thanks to many healthcare professionals, I will soon be able to start work again. My lungs are likely to be permanently sensitive to pollution and other irritants, but as long as I am careful, I will be able to return to cities, as before.

This book is the result of these walks in the mountains of northern Italy and southern Switzerland. I've walked at sunrise, in the sweltering heat, in mid winter. I've watched the seasons change, the baby boar grow into adults, seen the effects of pollution, and watched the effect of human carelessness when half of the mountain burned in forest fires. I've met foxes, deer, bats, owls, falcons, woodpecker, snakes, lizards, buzzards, porcupines, owls, and many other animals. I have rediscovered my love of the 'wild', with my trusty wolfdog, Dante, at my side, when he's not busy chasing the animals away.

I've followed the changes in the business world from a distance, while reconnecting to the natural world at a depth that I had forgotten was possible. I've been reflecting on the place of corporations in the world, on the very nature of business, and how we all need to change in order to be prepared for a future which must be much more environmentally connected. I need to walk again. This stone marker is getting a bit painful, and my legs are going numb.

My wild hike, traversing the mountain, took a strange turn when I stumbled across a mountain maintenance road. As usual, in Switzerland, no matter how remote the location, there's always a military installation and a maintenance road. I decided to follow the beaten path for a while to gain altitude faster. I've stopped at a little waterfall, further up the mountain.

It's not very easy to explore any more. Stepping off the known paths just leads to another path. We have maps for the whole globe, GPS coverage, Google, instant communication from anywhere in the world. I have perfect internet coverage here in the mountains, with faster connection speed than my WiFi at home. The irony of it all: these days you have to know an area of the world really well before you can go exploring, because it's almost all been mapped already. Walking for the last hour, I've been acutely aware that the small paths that I have been following most likely started out as wild animal tracks. Over centuries, they've been walked by many, marked, mapped, maintained, signposted. Walking in the mountains in Switzerland is almost more of a consumer than explorer experience.

I remember my teenage years fondly, running off the paths, through the woods, stumbling across escarpments, cliffs, waterfalls, and heading off into the mountains to really explore. No map, no compass. Just some food, clothes, and a pair of running shoes. I never liked hiking boots much. I found them too restrictive, and I ended up slipping more in them than I did in running shoes. So I ran, walked, scrambled through the middle of the woods, knowing full well that there were signposts, paths, tourist cafés, and much easier ways to do it. I ignored the signs, choosing the harder and more rewarding path, where I might meet a fox, or a chamois, or find mushrooms and wild berries. Now, I gently pick my way through the most interesting parts of the woods, remembering what it is to be off the map, exploring a bit. With Google in my pocket, so I can get back in time to collect Brendan.

I couldn't really be here without many generations of work. The men who carved the road into the hill, those who cut the tunnels and passes that allowed me to drive here, the local villagers who have maintained the lower paths for centuries, the woodsmen who maintain the mountain so that it's less dangerous to access. I'm relying on the work of literally hundreds of people in order for me to do a little 'exploring' of nature in this moment. I both love and hate that. I would prefer to be a 'proper' explorer, off all known maps, with no backup or safety net, testing myself against nature. There's something deep in me that needs to explore, needs to roam and discover, and make my own paths, discovering things that nobody else has ever seen. I think there's something deep within all of us that needs and wants that. That's the essence of this book: a desire to acknowledge the past, but to look beyond the known, beyond received wisdom, beyond everything we know about what it is to be in business. Onwards and upwards.

Exploring takes longer. It's 12.30, three hours since I left the car. The hiking guide said it would only take one and a half hours to the peak. Google says I'm only half way. I guess it's measuring for fit, healthy people, who aren't carrying a laptop and stopping to work. The climb feels interminable, and I'm getting out of breath every twenty minutes or so. That's part of my plan. I need to gently push myself physiologically to the limits of my lung capacities so that they can continue their recovery process. It's exhausting work, and I've been at it for about two years. My body is starting to respond, building more strength and lung capacity. A year ago, I wouldn't have been able to walk even 100 metres uphill. Today, I'm aiming for 6km of uphill work. I'm at a decision point. Do I continue to meander, and risk not getting to the top of the hill, or do I stick with that target, and lose the capacity to explore? It's a tough decision. I really want to reach the top, but I don't want to lose the exploratory quality of my walking. I will try to balance the need for efficiency with my need to experience more natural, flowing ways of being.

Any time we enter uncharted territory, we need to slow down, take in more information, be more careful, less efficient. There are no straightforward choices when there is no path. Aspects of this book will be a new experience for you, the reader. A business book that doesn't immediately get to the point, that demands pause for thought, that doesn't give you, the consumer, exactly what you want immediately? I can hear you thinking… "I've paid for this; it should at least do what it says on the cover". Welcome to the world of the exploring mindset. If you can allow the frustration, settle into a rhythm, and allow the story to unfold, it will reward you in very surprising ways. If not, well, that would mean

that I've not been genuine in my explorations of the subject matter. I would value that feedback. So, sit back, get comfortable, and allow the metaphors to shake up your thinking a bit. Did that sound creepy? Sometimes I wonder what I'm thinking when I write things like that. Maybe this is where I need to give a disclaimer: I've worked in executive coaching and studied various forms of psychotherapy over the years, so this book is likely to be slightly mind-bending.

Don't apologise for being yourself;
apologise for the pain you cause.

I want to apologise for any feelings of frustration, irritation, or anger that you, the reader, may be experiencing through engaging with this book. I am trying to be as succinct as possible. This may be edited out by my editor. I hope not, as I think it's core to the idea of building a human business. Surely I need to make things in a way that feels right to me, even if I irritate people sometimes? "But frustration about reading a book that says it's about business and love, but doesn't get to the point… how can that be useful?", you may ask. Dear reader, I thank you for your patience. Please, keep reading. It will unfold eventually. I expect it will all magically fall into place at some point, like the mushroom stew at the end of a walk in the woods.

You may be wondering at this stage whether I will ever get to the point, or whether this entire book will simply consist of meandering through forests, in an extended metaphor about life, business, and efficiency.

Learning to walk again

My intent isn't to meander. It is to find a connection to purpose which reaches beyond our current ways of thinking and structuring organisations. If meandering thoughts aren't your thing, that's ok. But at this stage, I don't know how this book will turn out, any more than I know what decision I will make about whether to follow a track in the woods or not. What I *do* know is that if you choose to ignore exploring and meandering in your life and business, your organisation is very likely to suffer catastrophic consequences over the coming years. You will have to read this book to discover more of my thinking on that. And sorry, no, there's no neat chapter title for you to look for. This book is an exploration, with some signposts. It's not a completed map.

Note for the curious: I've decided to follow the maintenance path for now, as I will get to the summit sooner, and I really want a photo of the view. I can also type notes while I walk. Ironically, in order to achieve a goal, I've stepped off my own exploratory path for a moment so that I can explain how necessary exploring is. I just smelled mushrooms; off into the woods. Yeah. I changed my mind again.

My pulse is 144. I've reached my cardio limit. I'm not at the top. My brain is getting fuzzy. I knew that I might not reach my target, as I was testing my lung endurance. I will have to turn back soon. Some would call this failure. Or poor planning. I call it an experiment. I wanted to test how far I could get towards a target. I wanted to explore a new woodland. I wanted a photo from the top of the mountain. But I also chose the tougher path, found some mushrooms, discovered a road that's not on the map, wrote three chapters of a book, and took lots of photos. Exploring means that we sometimes don't reach the target that we set. We learn, adapt, discover things as we go along. The next time we're in the same territory, we'll make more progress. I apologise for the lack of photo from the top of the mountain.

Sometimes goals are better abandoned.

But what about business? What if corporations lived within their limits, our limits, the limits of the ecosystem? What if they remembered what it is to love, to meander, to explore, to just try things, and see what happens, to experiment, push limits in a gentle and caring way? What would that look like? Would we be comfortable abandoning targets? Letting go, because the process was one our company learned a lot from? Do we have to plan everything ahead? Does it all have to be about achieving our targets? What is the goal that had you reach for this book? What's the direction you're heading in? Do you have time to meander, to explore new areas, new kinds of business? Is there enough leeway in your plans that failure is allowed? If not, the days of your business are likely numbered. Why such extreme language? The world has changed. I'm working, while hiking in the mountains, while writing a book. The old models of workplaces are defunct. The old model of what it is to be a business is dead. I can work *while* recovering from ill health, not waiting for my physio sessions in an airless room to be over, but walking in the hills, taking my time, exploring what my limits are, pausing for breath, and gathering my thoughts.

Well, I made it to the first peak, but not the one I wanted to get to. I rested, wrote some more, and pushed as hard as I could to get there. My body and legs are shaking, and my lungs are at their limits. Pulse 110, if you are interested. I'm completely out of breath. I managed to complete a four hour uphill walk. Altitude 1447m. For every bit of exploring, I had to work harder to achieve my goal. I had to compromise. I had to change my target slightly, to head to a different peak. But I learned something about my physical limits, about the joy and love of exploring, and the importance of focus and target orientation when it's needed. I also realised that my definition of love is actually the same as my definition of creativity, spirituality, and exploring: it's all about searching for the awe-inspiring in each moment. But 'Awe-inspiring Incorporated' doesn't have the same ring to it.

The Swiss are quite a savvy nation. They're as consumerist as it gets, but with a respect for nature. Here, near the top of the mountain, there's a hut. It serves fresh food, drinks, and sells cheese and dried meats produced on the premises, and with a fancy branding and online store. This is the home of the legendary 5 franc Coke. Someone had to bring it up the mountain, and I am expected to pay for that. It's the price of accessing this amazing scenery. After four hours of hiking to get here, it's a very tempting proposition, but I'm going to stick with my water taken directly from a spring.

Finally, I reach the top of the mountain. It was gruelling. Exasperating. Sweaty. I don't have time to stop other than to catch my breath. But I do have time to hop quickly with one foot on either side of the Italian-Swiss border. On one side, one set of laws applies, on the other, a different one. On one side, if I fall and break a leg, I will be rescued free of charge, on the other, I'll have to pay the helicopter and ambulance fees. On one side, peace apart from animals and insects. On the other, the industrial machinery maintaining mountain paths. I dig up a mountain cyclamen, to take home to Mary. It is exactly on the border line, so there is no jurisdiction that would cover the act of natural vandalism.

I'm not torn at all between the two countries. The Italian philosophy of nature suits me much better. There are wild animals everywhere, wolves have been reintroduced, bears are still present, and the approach to management of forests is minimalist. No warning signs about cliffs, very few distance markers. It's like risk managers and actuaries haven't been allowed in the mountains. I value enormously the Swiss design philosophy, and their efficiency. They make things to last, plan every detail, leave nothing to chance. Their engineering is second to none. But somehow, in their desire to 'master' the natural environment, they've rendered it impotent. It's just another thing to consume, along with your 5 franc Coke.

That paradox, how to carry efficiency and exploration, nature and nurture, wildness and tameness, lies at the heart of the future. Somehow we need to find ways to live in, and with, the environment, not only exploiting it for our gain. We need to learn from the Swiss and from the Italians. Rationality and feeling. Logic and emotion. Integration, not separation. The future isn't about sitting in circles singing *Kumbayah*, as an antidote to the excesses of consumerism. It's about finding songs we can sing in our organisations, songs that have meaning and intent, that show respect for nature in all its wild and awe-inspiring beauty. It's about loving the people, the planet, the animals, the environment more than we love money and power.

The business of the future is an overtly spiritual one, one which takes into account the whole, not only the part that we think we understand. It's about going off the beaten track, finding new ways of doing things we've been doing for hundreds of years, and doing them with more care and attention to the impact on the world around us. Having said that, if I ever need surgery, I want to have it in Switzerland. And when I want a pizza made with love, I'll head to Italy.

While walking, I decided to pass my first draft by Mary. She's an editor, with an amazing gift for getting right to the heart of what matters in writing. She said "I think it will all fall into place… and that it can't happen until you get to the end, and know you are there." Those words are now bouncing around in my head. It's like an exhortation to trust my process. I'll just know when it *clicks*. It's starting to click, now that I'm incorporating her edits, and starting to make decisions about the formatting. I'm starting to get a better sense of how all of this might work. It's quite complicated, because it's not linear, not purely logical, and not simply a flight of imagination, either. It's a *whole* that has parts, and all of the parts have to somehow fit together in a magical kind of way that leaves it feeling like a book, rather than a series of fragments.

It's Friday, the last day of Brendan's work experience with surgeons in Lugano. Each day this week, I've been going on trips in the area, working from my laptop, and thinking and feeling my way through what I want to say in this book. On Monday I wanted to sit in a café to write. I drove to the centre of Lugano, and realised that the parking would cost me 20 francs, and I would then have to pay an exorbitant amount to have a table for the day. So I decided to find a picnic table in the shade. I looked online, and none of the picnic areas seemed very inspiring to me, so I drove up to the top of a mountain, Monte Ceneri, where I remember that there are tables. Sadly they were all in full sunshine. It's the end of August, but the sun is still too strong. So, having driven for 30 minutes, with clear alpine air, I went for a walk to decide what to do next. I wandered past a herd of cows, bells clanging too loudly for me to think, so I continued until I couldn't hear them any more. Next, the sound of the motorway. I took a path that looked interesting to me, and followed a wild animal track. Swiss soldiers, shooting high velocity rounds, shattered the silence. I was irritated; I wanted peace and quiet. I looked at Google, and saw a side of the hill facing away from the firing range, away from the cows and away from the motorway, hundreds of metres below. I decided to walk there, traversing the side of the mountain through the woods, to see if there were any mushrooms.

Three hours later, I reached the side of the mountain

that was peaceful. Glorious silence. Punctured by crickets, streams, and the occasional helicopter. I sat for a while, pondering how hard it was to find peace, escape from the busyness (ironic, isn't it, that business is the same word, spelled differently), and bustle of life. Having reached a peaceful place, I didn't have any time to sit and write, or meditate, or accomplish what I set out to do. I had to find the fastest way back to the car, or I would be late to collect Brendan. So I scrambled up the side of the mountain to the peak, pushing myself physically to my limit, and discovered an unmarked military road, which quickly took me back to the car. After walking 15km in search of inspiration.

Following our instincts can lead to profound insight, but only if they are sharpened first.

In the process of trying to find a peaceful place to sit and write, I rediscovered something profound. My love of exploring in the woods, with no plan, no destination, but with a clear concept of the experience that I wanted to have. I rediscovered what it is like to be in flow, in the moment, physically testing myself against nature, and how it feels to really explore a terrain for the first time. I decided to change my plans for the week, and to search for inspiring locations to sit and work, allowing the process to unfold. Tuesday, I walked 5km, along a river, up the side of a hill I had wanted to drive up, to the border between Italy and Switzerland. The road that Google suggested was actually closed to cars, so I took a walk in the woods instead. No writing. Just mulling how hard it was to find anything I was looking for. Wednesday, it was raining all day. I sat in the car, high in the mountains, wondering why the forecast was so different to the weather. I decided to spend the day doing paperwork using the perfect 4G reception. Thursday, I went hunting for peace again, and climbed *Denti Della Vecchia*. Finally, some writing. Ironically, while walking.

Today, Friday, I'm hunting again for a place to sit, preferably by a mountain stream. I decided to not buy sparkling water at the supermarket. Instead, I'm on a hunt for wild water, spring water. Pure and fresh, straight from the mountain. And maybe a place to make a dam. Why? I'll tell you after I've found it. I need to drive some more.

Oh, by the way, last night I wondered how this book would end up looking. I had already designed the cover, and decided what size I'd like it to be, and approximately how thick. I want it to be 9-11mm, something that's chunky enough to feel solid, but not too hefty. That means I will need around 160-180 pages of text. I quickly edited the writing I did, leaving a total of 3500 words, and placed it in a draft design. 13 pages. So I have to write about ten times that much to get to a book that's the size I would like it to be. I felt immediate relief. This plan is taking shape. Ten more days of writing. Now I know the size of the arc that I'm aiming for, this will all be easier. While walking yesterday, I imagined gritty black and white photos scattered through the book, you know, like old halftone newsprint photos. I'll take photos with that in mind, and see what I can make of them.

I'm editing, designing, testing, typesetting, and

writing, all interleaved, rather than writing a full manuscript, then editing, then handing it to an editor, typesetter and cover designer. Quite unorthodox, but it's how my creative process works best. I tend to start with a general picture of the outcome, and the details gradually emerge, all together. I think most people work this way, but for whatever reason, that's not how we believe things should be done. The reason that books aren't usually made this way is because in the past, the process was *extremely* labour intensive. Nobody could possibly have done the job of a typesetter and writer. Nor that of a designer and writer. They were mutually incompatible, because a typesetter had to work physically with blocks of metal, on a flat table, and a designer with pencils and paint on an angled surface. The world is changed, thanks to personal computing. Of course, purists would say that my typesetting is poor, and my design is lacking finesse.

> *Any time we gain something, we lose something: that's just life. Best to accept it; the universe isn't going to change just for us.*

But that's the essence of change: we always lose something for the amazing things that we gain. Now I need to find a way to deal with these little 'asides'. Footnotes, perhaps. Or maybe grey boxes, with rounded corners. Oooo. I like these grey boxes. I'll stick with these. Hmmm. I'm writing this a day after writing the beginning of this paragraph. I wonder if readers will notice. I'll get Mary to check that there's no inconsistency of voice, so I can hide it.

Never mind. I just deleted the grey boxes, three days later. I needed the clarity for a while, so that I could work out how to deal with my different 'voices'. It turns out that I don't need to make anything simpler than it is. I just wrote the Gadfly principles section, and it has really helped me to realise that it's ok for the text to be self-contradictory, confusing, complex, *human*. I added gaps, grouping paragraphs together, to allow for deviation from the narrative. That has somehow given me a sort of permission to erase the grey boxes. I actually needed them for *me*, not for *you*.

Sometimes roads need to be closed. I'm trying to get to my mountain stream, but the road is being repaired. I'm stopped at a traffic light, with a wait of 15 minutes. Perfect roads come at a price. Many of the drivers are out of their cars, talking about a herd of deer that has been hanging out all year in the valley below. The foreman of the works is local, and says its very rare to see them down from the mountain, and quite worrying. The light turns green, after a magical moment of insight into the paradoxical Swiss relationship with nature. Everyone knows that the road needs to be maintained, or their livelihoods will be at risk. So they're patiently waiting. No complaining. No irritation. Simply accepting the price of living in a remote location.

Enforced sitting, waiting for the light, triggers a little insecure moment for me. What if I'm wasting too much time? I want to get to a stream. What if this is sounding more like a travelogue than a business book? What if people get bored of the journey I'm on? The feeling of pressure to deliver something of value is an interesting one to live with, while writing. I have to allow it, but not allow it to interfere with my process. If I was doing this whole thing the 'conventional' way, instead of following my instincts about streams, I would have identified the best location from a map, and gone directly to it. And I would be irritated at the wasted time sitting at this traffic light, waiting for Mario, or whatever his name is (he looks and acts like a Mario) to give me the green light.

> *Our story is the key to deep learning:*
> *ignore it, and we lose our wisdom.*

I find comfort in Mary's words from yesterday; a reminder to follow my instincts. My instinct says that this valley, *Calanca*, will have what I'm looking for today. It has the right kind of rock formations, stone, trees. I am slowly remembering my deep instinctual understanding of the Swiss mountains, and it's overwhelming to be reminded of that. I've inadvertently moved away from that as a way of being in life. I pass the digger, now moved off the road. The driver is sitting in the sun, earbuds in, hands behind his head, smiling. I assume its about how amazing it is to have work that only allows him to work for 15 minutes before having yet another break, sunning himself, watching the deer in the valley below. It's an unusually inefficient job for Switzerland.

Any project I do, whether business, personal, or creative, I start by imagining the end product. In this case, I wanted to write a book that would pop off the shelves in the business section, be visually arresting, while exploring the philosophical basis of my work in

Gadfly, and its application in organisations. I imagined a startling cover, with bold words on it. Something like 'Creative Business Ninja'. Something that stops people in their tracks, and attracts sales. I designed a cover, and gradually realised that I had created yet another clichéd business book. As I dove deeper into my own personal philosophy, I realised that I'm actually on a mission to create a deeply *spiritual* corporation, a business that's driven by love, creativity, human spirit, as well as profit, effectiveness, and delivering on targets. I settled on the working title of 'Love, Incorporated'. Sharp, incisive, and different.

> *Separating the known from the unknown*
> *creates artificial clarity; an artificial divide.*

While designing a new cover, I reached a point where something didn't click. I had a city skyline, with a sort of sunrise behind it. The words 'Love' and 'Incorporated' were fighting with each other in my head. I don't want to incorporate love. I don't want to capture it and bottle it, and contain it in a legal structure. I want to create an organisation that allows love to flow and weave its way through a profitable and effective consultancy. At scale. I was struck by a sudden thought; love is a core part of *The Future of Business*. Without it, we're only creating profit, building machines that will destroy our environment, ourselves, our world. I was walking at the top of *Campo Dei Fiori*, when I realised that the title was wrong. I was watching the sun go down behind the hill, hoping to see some deer coming out after dusk. I realised that the thing the cover was missing was nature. I took a photo, and rushed home to add it. As much as you can rush down a single track mountain road.

The mountain on the cover is one that I've walked hundreds of times. I know it inside out. I love it. I know where the fox lair is, where the owls have nests, where the deer hang out at different times of day. I've tracked wild boar, and met one that flung itself across the path in front of me as I walked, trying to escape my attention. It's a place where I feel truly connected, to myself and the environment. I kicked myself for trying to create a cover without it. After adding it, I cried. It felt *right*. I wrote down these words: "I never expected to cry about a business book." I immediately realised that this is *the* problem with business. The idea that it's ok for a large portion of our waking lives—around 35%—to not be personal, to not be human, is ludicrous. The idea of leaving emotion out of it is simply crazy. The idea that money and efficiency are somehow more important than our experience, than living, than the environment, than everything else… it's pure folly. So, I continued writing from that place: allowing my personal story, my mess, my emotion to be present, and setting my sights on weaving all of it together. My life, my story, my experiences, philosophy, approach to business—all of them need to be here.

Another traffic light, this time at the end of a gallery. Ok, now I'm really irritated. I just want to find a stream. I'm actively thirsty, too. The temperature is rising, as the sun comes over the mountains. It will soon be over 30 Celsius, with baking sun. But here I am, sitting waiting for workmen to finish rolling a new section of road. I've also just got email from Richard Merrick, my 'provocateur', in response to my writing from yesterday: "the world doesn't apologise to us when we get irritated if we don't understand it. Why should you?" I feel a wave of rage shooting through me. It's clear that he didn't understand the psychological techniques I'm carefully weaving into my writing, and he is projecting his bias. I don't need feedback like that. If I listened to him, I would risk the delicate thread that I'm trying to weave through, helping you, the reader, to be more open to new concepts than you might otherwise be. Thanks to Richard's provocation, I now have to reveal my 'trick', leaving you potentially no longer trusting me. Of course, I could edit this paragraph out, but then I wouldn't be honouring my intent, which is to write honestly and openly about my experiencing during this process.

Best to understand and own our beliefs,
or we risk projecting them on others' behaviours.

Human minds are strange places. We carry very fixed beliefs about the world and about people, most of them constructed around our fears, or the fears of people that we grew up around, which somehow seeped into us. Richard seems concerned that I am somehow putting too many disclaimers in the book, like my comments apologising if I irritated you. I think he's probably seeing that as a sign of 'weakness', or a lack of belief in my own truth, a lack of trust in my process. It isn't. It is a careful attempt to include you, the reader, and to weave around the objections you may have to being provoked in the way that I am aware this writing may provoke. Why apologise for irritating people? I sent him this reply: "Because I'm *human*. And being human is, at its core, about *relationship*. Besides, the apology is a way of undermining ego defences; no point leaving people stinging without saying 'that's not my intent... I'm simply trying to honour my own process here'. So, my query to you would be why would you care so little about how other people feel in contact with your process? :)"

The battle has begun. We're both experienced executive coaches and leaders of change. We have different blind spots, and different capacities. But now my book has been changed, and my method exposed. And now you, the reader, might not trust me any more. What do I do about that? And what do I do about the feeling of having my creative process messed with? And my philosophy challenged, while I'm trying to weave some delicate threads together here without you realising what I'm doing? I know what my other teenage son, Tristan, would say, with his acerbic insight. "He's such a Boomer, Dad; he wouldn't understand". 'Boomer' is his shorthand for someone who only thinks about themselves and money, creating disasters for everyone else: or anyone over the age of thirty that he disagrees with.

I'm irritated, thirsty, and just want to get to my stream. And I don't even know where it is. Damn me and my crazy exploration of exploring. I have a Skype call scheduled with Richard in 30 minutes. I'm tempted to find a corner with no signal. Now I'm laughing, and wondering how crazy you're thinking I am. I'm not going to apologise for that. Richard told me not to. Maybe I should. Now I'm doubting myself. I pass the whole exchange by Mary, she responds simply with "Honey works better than vinegar—Nanny". Her grandmother was a wise woman, and I think Mary is right; soothing egos is important. I remember Mary's words about everything falling into place, and mine feels calmed. Time to find some water. I'm still tempted to switch my phone off.

Just as I think I've got to the end of the valley, parked the car, surveyed the landscape and decided the direction I need to go in, ten minutes in to my walk, over a ridiculously trendy bridge, I come across a road that wasn't signposted. I *know* it's the right one; it winds under the big rock at the end of the hanging valley. It will lead somewhere magical. I head back to the car. Another twenty minutes wasted. As I jump into the car, eager to get to my stream, I hit my knee, and into my mind pops the detailed discussion I had yesterday with Brendan about leg vein and artery rupture, and how easily it can happen. Now I'm hoping I don't have to get airlifted to hospital, where he's observing in the emergency room.

One of the things when you head towards the 'wild', is that phone signal drops. The moment I turned the corner into the hidden valley, signal disappeared. Right when Richard called. I turned back, on foot, walking to the signal, and we had a brief conversation. He's going to stay out of the way of my process. I had to climb a rock to get signal, and was acutely aware of how different the experience is, age 48 to age 18. Fear of going to the edge. At 18, I would have sat with my feet off the edge, 20 metres above the road, swinging them in the wind. It's a good location for a Skype call, though. Richard thinks that my writing so far may be too meandering for some, and that might get in the way, but he also thinks the metaphors are rich and useful, and he's looking forward to where it goes from here. Given that he's an ex-CEO, my target market, I suspect that I'm on the right track. He's a bit unsettled, but not actively scared yet. That's the response I was hoping for. I won't send him this section for a while. Wouldn't want to trigger his inner 'Boomer'.

So, reader, the quest continues. Phone charged, backpack, notebook and pen. Empty water bottle in hand. Marmots scurrying away as I walk along the road. Off to find some magic. Thankfully my knee is better; no need for an airlift. Reader, I have to apologise again for how long it's taking me to get to the point, even though Richard says it's a bad idea to apologise. My meandering is even starting to frustrate *me*. I don't want to write a travelogue, but it feels like I'm on a really important journey here, both for myself and for you. I want to make sure I'm paying attention, noting my thoughts, and not missing anything. I'm gathering hundreds of subtle threads of my experience here. It will take some time, and I know that there is value for you in me writing this way, even if it's not yet clear to you. If you're bored, you could maybe skip to the end of the book. I expect it's likely to leave you wanting to come back here, though. Exploration that has any depth really has to be careful, meticulous, and slow. Like a surgeon, delicately teasing apart muscle from nerve from viscera, I have to tease apart my experience to get to the nuggets that are hidden deep inside. I wish I could do it faster, but there's a process we have to go through together, you and me. Now I feel like apologising for apologising. More time gone, and I still don't have any water.

I'm wondering whether the previous paragraph should be part of the main text, or a note. I've decided it should be in the main text, because it's a core part of the experience of writing the book, not a commentary on the process. But it's important to separate process from commentary. Now that Richard has 'intruded' into the writing process, it feels like that story is part of the main book. I'm aiming for emotional accuracy here, and am making rules, as I go along, about how to represent it, so that you can follow it. When we improvise, and create 'on the fly,' we have to be careful to separate the story from the commentary, the act of creating from any analysis of what we're creating. Otherwise, we end up criticising ourselves, and not creating freely. I guess it's a bit like the 'suspending judgement' part of brainstorming sessions. Theory: I'm trying to keep my judgements separate. Let's see if that holds true as the book progresses. In some therapy methods, this would be called the 'observer position'. It's important to be able to somehow separate ourselves from what we are creating, so we can look at it with more objectivity.

> *Sometimes we don't know what we need*
> *until we find it; no matter how certain we feel,*
> *it's best to be open to exploring.*

At the end of the single track pothole-ridden road, there's a land of giant one metre high ant hills, unspoilt forests, and crystal clear glacier water. I see marmots, butterflies, and hear the sound of streams and the river at the bottom of the valley. The only human marks here are the military road to the shooting range, and the occasional red and white striped tree, marking the hiking paths. I'm in the right place. Finally. Isn't it ironic: to write a book about the future of business, I've had to spend 5 days searching for somewhere remote enough to feel what I needed to feel?

As a child, I spent the summers high up in the Alps in a place called Adelboden. We lived in Switzerland when I was too small to remember, and after leaving, we visited each summer, staying with the Affolter family. Georges was like a grandfather to me. He and I spent hours walking in the forests. He taught me the way of the mountains. *Essor* was the largest watch and parts factory in the village. Georges was the director and owner. He wasn't a very conventional boss. He was generous and kind, and laughed and joked with employees. He prided himself on being a father figure to them. He loved showing me around the factory, and having me guess what the parts were for. They made some for NASA, and had clients around the world. The thing that Georges was *amazing* at was *being human*. He cared for his employees, cared about the village, cared about nature. He was an elder in the church that my Dad was the minister of, both when I was a toddler, and later when I was a teenager. He carried his faith very lightly, and was more Deist in his beliefs than Christian: his true love was, as he would put it, "communing with nature". So when he wasn't flying around the world, selling the benefits of 'Made in Switzerland', he spent most of his time in the mountains, picking berries and mushrooms, fishing, grilling chicken on fires in the woods, and hiking in the mountains. He brought his conviviality and spirit back into his work, and his factory's meticulousness into his chicken preparation.

Every year of my childhood, I went hiking with him. I learned about the best places to find blueberries, how to make jam, to read the lay of the land, the pattern of trees, the best places to see wildlife, and learned about the sheer joy of being part of the natural Alpine wilderness. As he grew too old to walk in the mountains, he sat on the balcony of his chalet, reading, and sharing his life philosophy, which he summarised as "*La confiture, c'est la vie*", Jam is Life. His day started with crusty thick cut toast, with fresh butter from the local dairy, and freshly made yoghurt, made from local milk, with jam that he made from mountain fruits.

His philosophy was simple: enjoy what life has to offer, and never take a single moment for granted. He carried his wealth and his power very lightly. It's only sitting here, at the end of the valley at the end of the valley, that I can feel how profoundly his way of life touched me. I eat toast and yoghurt with jam for breakfast, and pick wild fruits whenever possible. I'm a convert to Georges-isme. His philosophy was one of *love*. Above anything, love. Love nature, love people, love those who are close to you, love those who aren't. He stuffed chicken with pine needles and mountain herbs *with love*. He drove his Jaguar up the mountain passes *with love*. He taught me how to dam mountain streams *with love*. And he ran his business *with love*. Love for precision. Love for his staff. Love for his customers. Love for the valley. And gratitude for his position in life, having inherited and grown a business that went back generations.

There was a dark side to his story. During the war, the Swiss supplied the Nazis with parts for their weapons and machinery, and the factories in the valley supplied them with diplomatic bags full of valuable precision engineering without asking about the origins of the gold with which the Germans paid. Knowing that his wealth and opportunity had its origins in the suffering of millions of Jews left Georges, and his family, wracked with guilt. They, as many Swiss, gained enormous wealth as a result of the war: profiting from the suffering of others, while maintaining a stubbornly neutral stance. Whatever his motivation, whatever the pain he carried, it is his capacity to run a business, and live his life with love, that have stayed with me. He and my Father didn't see eye to eye on many things. My Father is a harsh Presbyterian type, who doesn't see the value of deep connection with nature, and found people like Georges to be 'simplistic', and 'theologically weak'.

So here I am, sitting by an alpine stream, realising what I want the future to hold. I knew I had to find a deeply peaceful place, and I followed that instinct. And now I'm realising that the key to my understanding of The Future of Business was handed down to me by my Swiss 'grandfather'. I'm also realising that the moment I entered the business world, I inadvertently abandoned this philosophy in the ways that I ran my own business. Georges died a few years ago. Nobody told me about his

funeral; they thought I wouldn't care about a 101 year old man. I've discovered why I came here. Next, I need to find some water.

My phone is almost out of charge, my shoes are soaked, and my jeans ripped, but I am proud to let you know that I found both fresh spring water and made a dam in a mountain stream. There is something so rewarding about 'interfering' with nature—the power to change the course of a river, to move stones and change the world a little. I know that exercising that power will permanently change the course of the little stream. It will maybe eventually cut the gorge a little wider on the right side. The next storm will change most of it back, though, and my marks will most likely be erased. It's an amazingly simple thing to do, to change the course of a little river. 20 minutes, some hard work, and a little understanding of flow, pressure, currents. It struck me how similar it is to organisational change and system change. Remove the blocks to the direction of flow that we want, redirect some of the flow to the new, and block as much as we can of the old. And that left me pondering… what if the future of business is *love*? What would we need to remove? What would we need to redirect? What would we need to actively block in the way our businesses work? I built a small cairn in memory of Georges, to thank him.

When we reject a philosophy, without first creating a new one, we are doomed to repeat the past.

Over the last few months, I've been outlining my vision for Gadfly. I started off wanting to rebuild my company, but the more I thought about it, the more I realised that I had changed too much, my perspective is too different, and my ambitions have changed completely over the last few years. I started off wanting to build a new corporation, one that was more rooted in creativity and coaching than the average. Now, after months of prodding and mulling (thank you, Richard), I realise that what I want to build is a *spiritual* corporation. A large scale, publicly traded, business whose core purpose is not about profit, money, or the personal gain of the directors, investors, or staff. Instead, its value comes from long term thinking, from planning the future, and building new philosophies: like Chinese dynasties, built to last a thousand years.

We are leaving an era of religious dominance which has lasted thousands of years. In most western countries, religion is on the decline, along with its cultures, attitudes, and teachings. The philosophical seedbed in which corporations were grown is disappearing, and they are becoming more and more rudderless as a result. What has largely replaced religion is the unacknowledged religion of the masses—*consumerism*. When people feel bad about something in their lives, they no longer pray or go to see a priest—they *buy*. Purchasing fuels the desire for more, and offers a short-term reward. It triggers a dopamine hit, just as finding a source of fresh water does when you're thirsty. Except that one is about *survival*, and the other is about *urges*. If we indulge our urges, never learning self-discipline, they get bigger. Before we know it, our whole life is consumed with money, saving, and spending. Business, fuelled by developments in psychology, has tapped into this reward circuit in a ferocious way, driving consumer behaviour to greater and greater extremes. We have justified it as 'good for growth', and of course 'growth is good'… because… ummm… it's better than what was before. It's a closed loop philosophy that declares that growth is good because progress is good, and progress is good, because growth is good.

This is not the natural order. Nature is cyclical. We are born, we grow, we die. This is the case with any natural system. It's simply a *truth* of the universe. Exponentially growing consumption will, by definition, end. How? Probably by a crash of the whole system. When? Who knows. But it's worth thinking about, planning for, and preparing ourselves for emotionally. But we're like babies whose mothers have taken away their dummies, tantrumming and screaming about the loss of comfort, loss of ease, loss of convenience, etc. We need to get over it. We're not on this world to have easy lives. We need to change. We need to look far into the future, to a time when we live in harmony with the environment, when each organisation has a spiritual grounding, passing on deep wisdom, and understanding about living harmoniously with each other and our environment.

Gadfly aims to be the world's first truly spiritual corporation. Hopefully one of many. Our aim is to revolutionise the way business is structured and conducted. We aim to be human, loving, caring, responsible, and to encourage other businesses to follow our example, but to do it in their own ways. Because *Jam Is Life*.

Making my way back from the mountain stream, I feel at peace, like my relationship with the natural world is now in its rightful place, awe-struck by how small I feel, and overwhelmed with love for the mountains, and the wild raspberries I tasted. Back at the car, life just feels too noisy. The workmen are still laying the new surface. Cars on the motorway feel too fast. People seem like they are all stressed to their limits. It feels like being punched in the stomach. Maybe that's how far we are from where we need to be. Maybe we're all so stressed out, so driven by dopamine and adrenaline that we can't even relax until we're on holiday. I go to the grocery store, and am completely overwhelmed by the artificiality of the experience. No need to hunt for hours to find a mountain spring; the bottled water has pictures of mountains, neatly printed for our convenience on plastic wrap.

Too much certainty leaves no room for wonder, or longing.

No wonder I feel gut-punched. The world has gone crazy with the desire for *more*, and we call it 'normal'. There's nothing normal or natural about it. If anything, after spending the day in the deep mountains, lost in nature, everyone seems scared of not having enough, while surrounded by mountains of unnecessary luxury. The Beatles pop into my head: "I don't care too much for money. Money can't buy me love." The more we have, the less love we show, and the less we can feel it.

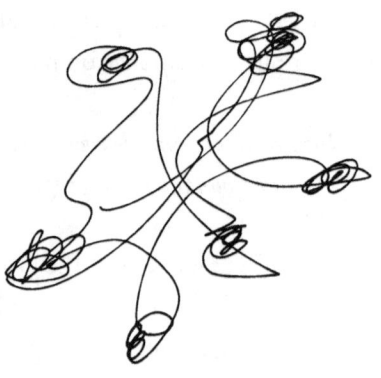

Everyday happenings

I'm in a 'queue' outside my barber's in Italy. He's having a post-lunch cigarette, after having two and a half hours off to eat with his family. Everyone has memorised their numerical position in the group, and they are all smoking, chatting, waiting for Daniele to finish his cigarette. I'm third in the hidden queue. Interestingly, people who visit Italy mostly don't seem to notice that queues here work this way, and often create the chaos that they imagine Italy to be. I drive thirty minutes, past maybe twenty barbers, to have my hair cut. I usually combine it with shopping in the area, and visiting friends, but I drive here for Daniele. Daniele is an old-school barber, trained in very traditional Italian techniques, but he has also trained in Turkish styles, contemporary cuts, and super sharp fades. He's the *Maestro* of the fade. In the last two years, his business has grown from just him in a small shop, to three barbers, with six or eight people waiting. Why has his business grown, while other traditional barbershops have shut down? It's almost all down to his love of music, and his love of really detailed, very sharp, graduated clipper hairstyles. He wanted to open a combined club/barbershop, where people could hang out to have their hair cut, have a drink, and spend the evening listening to Italian hip hop. Of course, Italian laws are too rigid for him to be able to have a "mixed" business like that, so he had to open a barbershop.

The thing is, his business isn't growing because of the branding, which is mostly tattoo-chic. It's growing because of *who he is*, because of his natural passions, and the things he cares about. He attracts the cool, trendy, mostly 20-somethings, who want a cut that's Instagram-worthy. In the back room, he has a photo background and lights, so he can post his latest work on social media, tagging customers, and gaining social traction. His barbers respond to social media messages within minutes, and people don't mind waiting in the shop, because it's a place they're proud to be seen.

Daniele's shop isn't something that can be faked. The barbers who are attracted to working with him are all super talented and creative, usually working in silence, all masters of 'the fade'. They're flexible, kind, and happy sharing the space. Daniele created a clear concept of what mattered to him, and invited others to join him. His wife runs the bookings for the busier weekend days, and his baby daughter is often in the shop, sitting on clients' knees. This is a *real* place, not a manufactured brand. We have often spoken about him starting a chain of shops. He would love to have one in London. I said that the issue is that he would have to visit regularly to maintain the same feel, to monitor the sense of what matters in the place, because that's what works about his business. That stuff can't just be canned, put into a brand strategy, or an advertising campaign. In essence, what he has done is to create a *high value brand*. It combines personality, music, superb detailing, and a calm confidence. Those are all of his personal attributes, which is what makes the place special, and the experience unique.

Over the years, corporate branding has attempted to replicate this high human-touch business model. We now have 'family businesses' with thousands of employees, 'genuine farm' products at industrial scale, and 'hand made' products made in sweatshops. With increasing automation, and particularly with the introduction of AI removing more and more of the 'human touch' from business, we are eroding what makes many businesses special. No matter what scale an operation, especially in the service sector, if the people aren't the experience, aren't present, and can't express themselves authentically, the business will under-perform. Simply because it lacks that 'feel', that 'thing': the *human* factor.

Love is the future of business, because at some level, we can all tell what is a manufactured experience, and what is a genuine expression of people's passions, interests, and obsessions. Just as we can tell the difference between an online profile and the real experience of an individual, we can see the difference between workers who truly value what they are doing, versus those who have been on a 'brand values' training course so they show 'aligned behaviour' for the purposes of 'client experience'. The future belongs to companies that can leverage technology at scale without removing the human, the personal, the passion, the love, from the experience. The reason Daniele doesn't have a shop in London yet? Because he doesn't want to be away from his baby. "Maybe when she's older". Family is one of the things that matters so much to him that I doubt he will ever open his London branch; he would have to compromise who he is, or the quality of what he offers, to be able to do it. He's not willing to do either. Love isn't an easy path, but the results are worth it.

> *We all need hierarchy and structure,*
> *but we need them to serve our needs.*

This morning, I'm walking with Dante on 'my' mountain, *Campo Dei Fiori*. I say with, but in reality, I'm walking, and he is chasing deer and wild boar, and peeing everywhere, so every animal knows how far his territory extends. Wolves walk up to 100km every day, marking their territory as they go. They systematically follow the edge of the territory, refreshing the markings on a regular basis. Dante does the same, and when I make sure that he goes to all of our regular spots, on a sort of rotation, he is much happier, and more chilled while walking. Wolves also have a strong social structure, and the male alpha has to be an overt leader, or others will challenge him. If I'm too nice to him, he starts to think that I'm losing my 'edge' as an alpha, and his behaviour becomes more aggressive.

So, if I put my head below Dante's, the first time he freaks out, acting like I've offended the 'natural order'. The second time, he will look weirdly at me, and the third, he will become aggressive with me, and begin the process of trying to take my place in the wolf pack. Regular scuffles are necessary to remind him of his place. It's quite scary, wrestling a half-wild animal that could bite through my arm, but it's a necessary part of respecting him. His need for a hierarchy initially upset me, as I personally value low hierarchy systems, but I've become more used to occupying the 'evil tyrant' position with respect to him. Learning his native language has helped me to see how natural the need for hierarchy is. Any human system that says hierarchy is artificial is simply in denial. We all *need* hierarchy.

I just had to stop writing, because a young, and ill disciplined, Labrador-pitbull decided to try to take Dante on, signalling dominance, tail in the air, baring teeth. The owners, who clearly can't read dog body language, decided that Dante was being aggressive, and started criticising me aggressively for allowing my dog to threaten theirs. I stood there calmly, with Dante making his yelping hunting call. I looked the owner in the eye, and said "he's responding to your dog's aggression". They turned and walked off, muttering about how it's not just my *dog* who is aggressive, with their dog snarling and snapping, while Dante cowered beside my knee. Humans are so stupid, sometimes. If you come across a wolfdog, be calm and gentle, and it will be the softest animal you'll ever encounter. Snap at it, and you may not live to tell the story. They're direct descendants of apex predators; why expect anything different? And if you're going to have a hard-to-handle dog, please learn how to manage it. Wolfdogs can't be trained like other dogs can. They're only half dog.

Now I've lost my thread. I was looking down on the industrial complex of northern Italy, thinking philosophical thoughts about efficiency. I'll leave it for another time: it will take a few hours to calm Dante.

I guess if there's anything to learn from this, it's that some people simply don't think about consequences, behaviours, or how they create difficulty for themselves and others. That's a perfectly valid reason to leave them lower in the human hierarchy than those who can think, reflect, ponder, and make decisions that have positive knock-on effects beyond their personal situation. Where would we be, if thoughtless self-interested people, unaware of, and uncaring about, their impact in the world, were at the top of the hierarchy, playing Russian roulette with the future? Hmmm. Perhaps it's time to rethink what we value in society.

If I had left Dante to his own devices, he would have either forced the dog to surrender, and accept a lower position in the hierarchy, or he would have asked my permission to kill it. It wouldn't have been personal; it's about the stability of the pack structure, about the well-being of everyone he cares about, and the safety of the territory.

That's not really so different to how human societies and organisations work. Brutal cost-cutting that doesn't take into account personal circumstances, 'downsizing' that is all about profit: it's all about hierarchy, and right at the top of the hierarchy is *money*, not humanity. We all have a bit of wild in us. And we need to get to know it, to nurture it, to explore it. Otherwise it ends up running us. Business isn't personal, after all.

Last month, I needed to drive half way down Italy, to Rieti, about six hours on the *Autostrada*. I looked at the route, and saw that it passed through amazing places like Cremona, Parma, Bologna, Perugia. I checked the toll prices (the *Autostrade* are privately owned), and discovered that the trip would cost me over €80. I wasn't wanting to line the pockets of the rich, and I had a few days of flex, so I decided to meander down the country, stopping to visit some of the towns. I decided to see how cheaply I could do the trip, so I drove really slowly, obeying the 50-90-110 speed limits to the letter, enjoying the slow unfolding of the country. Within a few hours of leaving home, I was ducking and weaving around small towns, with the help of Google. I realised that this journey was going to be a lot more complex than it would have been twenty years ago, before all of the towns had bypasses. At every turn, Google was taking me off the small roads, onto bypasses and dual carriageways. I had to stop repeatedly, trying to find the most interesting route. I ended up abandoning Google completely, instead writing down a list of the towns I wanted to head through, and trying to 'go analogue', to have a more inefficient, but more observational, experience.

It was an amazing journey, slowing down, no longer thinking in terms of getting from A to B. I decided to see where I ended up, to stop at a local roadside *trattoria*, and to find something local on Airbnb. I wanted to stop

Everyday happenings

for something to eat at Parma. I followed the city centre signs, and came across warnings about parking, and fines for driving in the city centre. Park-and-ride schemes weren't operational, so I stopped to look up how the city worked from a visiting point of view, reading the anti-pollution measures, and the parking plans. I realised that I would be risking a fine if I went anywhere near the centre at all. I looked for a *trattoria*, but could only find fast food. I decided to drive on to the next place. Parma seemed like a trap. Bypass led to bypass, led to bypass, led to bypass, each a maze of McDonalds, Burger King, strip mall, shopping centres, and randomly changing speed limits. I got lost occasionally, but only found more of the same: roundabouts, malls, and McDonalds. I eventually accepted that I would get lost, and ended up on country roads that led back to more bypasses and fast food. I gave up, and drove to the mountains, following Google directions, waiting to explore in a place that I knew there would be less 'charted' territory. I wrote this on the way:

Am I willing to be *lost*? Am I ok to take a less efficient path? Am I *really* willing to explore? Can I trust my instincts more than Google? Can I surrender to the experience of being? Suddenly I'm more open to my environment. My choices aren't right or wrong, rather interesting or not. I soon realise that there's so much ecological harm everywhere, that all choices feel a bit wrong. A choice between thirty different McDonalds. A choice between thirty malls. Strip mall all the way from Milan to Bologna. Interrupted by the smell of pigshit, because of the growing global demand for Parma ham.

The trip ended up taking twelve hours. I didn't see

any of the towns, because the traffic restrictions are so complex that it didn't seem worth the hassle, could lead to traffic violations, and parking is expensive everywhere. I wanted to stick to my 'low cost' plan. In my desperation for some sort of exploring, I drove up high into the Apennine mountains, up a little track, far above the little town of *Mercato Saraceno*. I decided to sleep in the car for a few hours before continuing my journey south. Finally, some exploring. I woke up at dawn with the most amazing view of the hills, mist rising, and the sun peeking between the cliffs. Worth the effort and discomfort. I decided to drive back on the motorway.

> *Money is just a tool; gather it wisely, or it will diminish our humanity.*

One month later, almost to the day, I've just received my fifth speeding ticket, sent out automatically by the local police. Total cost: around €300. Each of them was for between 2-4kph above the speed limit. Each was in a zone that I thought had a limit of 90, the national speed limit, but the limit was actually 80. Somehow I missed the special '80' signs, which don't exist in the area in which I live. I've lived in Italy for almost four years in total. I've never once had a ticket. In the thirty years that I've been driving, I've had *one* speeding ticket. I'm really good at seeing signs, and speed camera warnings, and I'm normally not a fast driver at all. I set out to drive slowly, and thought I was 10kph under the limit. But here I am, getting fines for being 2kph over the limit, which is lower than the human error reading a speedometer.

It's practically *Swiss*. Only the Swiss wouldn't be so judgemental about it, and would allow 10% error, where Italy allows 5%, which is the *technical* error, and doesn't allow for any of the human error of reading a dial. The Swiss also wouldn't send fines in green envelopes of varying shades, that neighbours and postmen sneer at, attempting to layer the guilt and shame so that I repent my 'transgression'. Yes, it's even called a *trasgressione* on the forms. The next time I drive south, I'm going to be a good little consumerist, plan everything ahead of time, and pay my €80 to one of the richest companies in Italy for the honour of driving on their roads. It turns out that exploring can be a very expensive thing to do, if you do it in the wrong places. The small consolation is that I have given money to some amazing little towns. I hope that the local police will use the money wisely; maybe they should invest it in the motorway company.

The Italy that I knew and loved, living here twenty years ago, has almost disappeared. It has been replaced by money-making machines, which have all but eradicated the joys of the old way of life. There are lots of benefits, though; I'm never more than about 10 minutes drive away from a quick 'hit' of fast food, or a giant store selling cut-price imported clothing so that I, too, can live the American dream. But I'm in *Italy*. Sometimes I really resent globalisation. There's no love in it; only profit, and it has shredded the cultures that I knew and valued. Oh, and an interesting statistic. Italy has 23,000 speed cameras, the third highest number in the world after Germany and Brazil. They bring in around €2bn of annual income to local government. That's one speed camera for every 2000 adults, and an average of one ticket per year per adult. €40 a head of easy money. The investment will pay off after about a year, and thereafter will be pure profit at around €80k per camera annually. The Post Office benefits, too; they get the extra €16 delivery fee, and the opportunity to sneer at customers. One *comune* in Italy boasted of recording 58,000 infractions in its first two weeks of speed trap operations. It's hardly surprising to me, as many of the speed limit signs are hidden behind unkempt roadside bushes. Most likely on purpose.

Flow is powerful: allow it, and magic happens; block it, and we lose our capacity to be present.

I was in Rieti to take photos of an international basketball tournament, for another of our books: *We Are Basketball*, a photo story about Italian youth basketball culture, and how the craft of becoming a champion is handed down from generation to generation. While taking photos, I met a few of the local pro photographers. I find it fascinating to watch others taking shots. Alessio, always looking for the creative angles. Alice, taking photos to connect, tagging players on social media. And Giulia, doing it for the dance: following every movement, present to what was happening on the court, always in motion. I ended up watching photographers as much as the basketball. Giulia's process reminded me of the magic of creating while in flow: that liminal thread of presence, process, and experiencing, that only come together in the moment. After watching her working, I knew I had to

Everyday happenings

write this book. We didn't have time to chat over coffee, so I'll return to Rieti some time, driving more slowly.

Yesterday I spoke with Pavel Golenistsev, a young organisational psychologist who is leaving the corporate world to set up his own business, focused on helping entrepreneurs to build purpose-led companies. He asked me to explain more about what I was aiming to do with Gadfly, and my vision of what a human corporation would look like. I found myself thinking about how difficult it will be to swim against the tide of corporate-driven consumerism. I had a brief moment of thinking that it might be better to build something small and local instead. There's always wisdom in those brief moments. A tiny doubt, a little fear, a chink of vulnerability, can be the key that unlocks deep insight. I used to be driven solely by scale, power, reach, and 'global impact'. It's only now that I've seen and felt my way through the sheer folly of that path, and the environmental carnage that we have created, that I'm able to see the depth of wisdom in 'small', and 'local', too. So why am I still interested in building a publicly-traded corporation? Why not just build a little niche consultancy, and deliver awe-inspiring local projects?

I believe that we are facing the end of the consumerist model that we have built. We need a new model, new structures, new maps, new philosophies. The old model was built on a 'pile it high, and rake in the profit' philosophy that relies on scale and global reach. The larger the market, the bigger the profit. We're reaching the limits of that system, in terms of running out of raw materials, having lowered the cost of production thanks to automation, having better decision-making through AI, outsourcing to third world countries, and building sleek, efficient global supply chains. In our headlong rush towards exponential 'growth', we have created a giant unsustainable system, most of which we will need to re-purpose in order to have any chance of preventing total system collapse. This would lead to pain and suffering at a scale that has never been seen in the world's history.

Every system has limits: the more we ignore them, the more we will suffer.

I'm a Physicist. No matter what else I have studied, I always come back to the basic principles of Physics. Any physical system has boundary conditions (physical limits) and core conditions (assumptions and starting conditions). Capitalism in its current form has boundary conditions which are hitting the limits of growth in almost every axis it's possible to measure. We've reached peak oil, peak pollution, peak consumption, peak coffee, peak efficiency, peak employee satisfaction, peak earnings, peak profit margins, peak almost everything. Any physical system which grows exponentially, as our global economy has, and which reaches its natural growth limits, has one of three trajectories: reaching a steady state, exponential decay followed by steady state, or collapse.

If you think about a simple system like a bacterial culture in a petri-dish, the growth medium would represent the available resources, the bacteria would represent the global population, and the size of the petri-dish represents the physical limits of the world. We are a culture which has reached the edge of the petri-dish, and we are talking about how to continue growing. The physical reality is that it's impossible, in a closed system, to continue to grow at the same rate. Something has to give. We will, no doubt, find some ingenious technological solutions to continue to grow for a while, but all we are currently doing is postponing the eventual decline. We will have to live with flatlining economies, crashing economies, or economies that bounce up and down between crashing and flatlining. That's simply the physics of it. No matter what choices we make, ultimately our economies depend on *reality*. Our food is a limited resource. Manufacturing materials are limited. Fuel is a limited resource. Land is limited. Hence our desperate hunt for renewable resources.

What does this have to do with Gadfly? Well, whatever the future holds, unless we crash the whole system, it's certain that corporations are here to stay. They are becoming more and more powerful, more and more efficient, more integrated into every single part of our life, to the extent that we barely notice them any more. They're rapidly becoming the core infrastructure of modern life, and of the future. But as they have grown in scale, influence and power, the philosophical models that they are using haven't been updated at all. Most corporations are essentially still running to mid-1800s thinking: divide and conquer. Build empires. Militaristic style empires, created to defeat and subdue, creating maximal efficiency, caring only about one thing:

profit. Need to destroy a forest? No problem, as long as it makes a profit. Our world needs a new model, with new initial and boundary conditions. There is no public company in existence that would do anything so foolish as to try out completely new operating models, new philosophies, new methods of working, tools, metrics, methods of management across a whole organisation. The only way is to *prototype* it. That's why we want to build a corporation. To prototype new ways of working, informed by psychology, taking into account spiritual, environmental, ecological, and human wellbeing, and paving the way for corporations of the future.

Gadfly PLC will be a radical experiment. One which, if it is successful, will become a blueprint for business in the future. We will explore and test new ways of working, which make room for humanness, frailty, vulnerability, imperfection, and love, without sacrificing too much efficiency, productivity, clarity of outcome, effectiveness, or profit. Our aim is to offer these blueprints, free of charge, to any business who wants them. Over time, we will dismantle our company, as we will have accomplished our work: to build future corporations which are fundamentally human. The only way that we believe we can do this is by *showing* that it is possible, by doing it ourselves so that we can then guide, support, shape, consult to and encourage others to do the same in their organisations, speaking from a place of experience. It will be paradoxically small *and* large, local *and* global, efficient *and* human. And it will be built on relationships, authenticity, and a genuine desire to leave the future a better place for all. Why do this? Because we love solving difficult problems, exploring new terrain, and this is the toughest that we can find: building corporations that genuinely care.

As I'm writing, I'm conscious of how many pages this book will end up having. I don't want to waste words, but want to feel like I have finished saying what I need to say. I'm aware that each word takes up space on a page, and each page takes paper, and each sheet of paper takes pulp, and part of a tree. By choosing to publish this book as a physical object, I'm making a conscious choice to destroy other objects. It will also take water, minerals, dyes, glue, plastic, cardboard, causing pollution, and creating waste. The brutal reality of being alive is that living is a *destructive* act. We can't create or live without destroying things, but we can try to minimise the harm that we cause, and ensure that what we create is *worthy* of the damage that we are causing, and is meaningful enough to humanity that the value of its existence is greater than what it is replacing. That's a mighty standard to live up to. I hope that my words are meaningful enough to warrant the destruction that they are causing, and that they can prevent some future destruction that doesn't have meaning, or love, or a worthy cause behind it.

So, why print it at all? I think that the act of pausing to think about the value of the materials you are holding is a worthwhile thing to do. There is value *beyond* money. Not so long ago, the paper you are reading this on was a tree, standing in a grove, watered, sprayed to keep beetles away, cut, transported, pulped, rolled, cleaned, pressed, dried, and cut into rolls. Thanks to modern printing methods, this book will only be printed when ordered, so there's not a pile of unsold stock. The minimum materials are being used. I personally believe that this book is worth the paper that it's printed on, though at the same time, I grieve the ways in which we are wasting and destroying forests and the wild places of the earth. So, again, I'm caught in a *paradox*. I want to create, to share, to make, to be alive, to be human, but I also want to minimise the harm that causes, without compromising on what it is to be me. So I'm planting trees each week, nurturing them, valuing them, walking in the woods, maintaining my connection with nature, so that I don't ever forget what is truly valuable: life itself.

> *Rain on windows connects us to nature.*
> *But the glass separates.*

It's now been almost a week since I was in the hidden valley at the end of Calanca, building a dam. The boys are back at school, and the end of summer is approaching fast. The trees on *Campo Dei Fiori* are starting to change colour, and the temperature is falling gradually. I'm starting to feel the clarity of my connection with nature receding, in spite of having been up the mountain every morning. I'm looking out at a storm rolling over it as I write this, but it's not the same as being in the truly wild places, where I feel small and insignificant, and feel and see nothing but the grandeur of the natural environment around me. Some part of me is grieving the loss of the connection I had last week, and wishing there was a way for me to live in that place, to be deep in nature every

day, and to not ever be stuck in traffic, grocery stores, or pressed so close to other people, cut off from the wilds. I think I'll head to the mountains tomorrow to get a top-up. I managed to go six days without it. I'm not sure why I'm saying that like it's an accomplishment. It's not; I don't even want to go a day without it. I just checked the weather forecast. It's due to rain all day tomorrow. I'm not sure I want to be in the mountains in the rain, all day. Maybe I'm not so committed to this 'natural' life as I think. The storm has hit the house. I feel more alive, hearing the rain lashing against the glass, shutters banging, thunder, and Dante howling, as he paces up and down, worrying about the thunder invading his territory. He curls his head under my knee, and settles.

I'm sitting watching pre-season training of the Pallacanestro Varese U18 basketball team, late on a Friday evening. Training is held in the *Palazzetto Oldrini*, a historic basketball arena, where legends of basketball have played since 1965. It is one of the smallest arenas in the league, seating just over five thousand, but it is probably the most well known. It was designed at the height of space mania, and looks like a brutalist flying saucer. But the architecture isn't the reason people come; it's to say they've "stood on the boards at Varese". They come for the history. The club was founded in 1945, part of a post-war plan to help young men to continue learning discipline, athleticism, and focus. It's a very special place. A kind of temple to basketball. It's a battle zone, a training ground, a place of historic significance. Varese won many national and international titles in the 1970s, producing some of the greatest names in basketball history, like Meneghin, Morse, Rusconi. The club itself is "built from the blood of old champions". Ex players from all decades hang out, are on the board, and are involved in coaching, training, and developing future talent. Local fans are ferocious, modelling themselves on, and naming themselves after, the 'do or die' attitudes of the infamous Varese trench fighters from the First World War, *The Arditi*. It's an honour to be able to come here, week in, week out, to watch Brendan as he develops into a high level professional athlete, and as he grows into a man.

Varese is known for is its passion for basketball. Children here dream of one day wearing the red and white jersey. Because of his height, people who meet Brendan on the street ask if he plays basketball. When he responds with "yes, for Varese", they stop in awe. "*The* Varese?" Of the hundreds who start off as young Varese players, by age 18 there are only 15 left; those who have potential to be the future stars of Italian basketball. From these, a few will go on to be international stars. But Pallacanestro Varese is in financial difficulty. Years of 'passion trumps money' have taken their toll on the club. Decades of 'but we are Varese' have left the club with few financial reserves, and their professional players are the lowest paid in the *Serie A*, the top league in Italy. Why? Because the club doesn't want big corporate sponsorships. They don't want the 'pure game' to be diluted, or the quality of their heritage to be reduced. They prefer to have sponsorship by hundreds of small local companies, a consortium that provides for their needs. 50km Away, Olimpia Milano, now known simply as *Armani*, has 'sold out' to the sponsors. Players earn millions, and the club can afford any luxury, with their annual budget of around €30 million. Varese, playing in the same league, with similar results, has a budget of €3 million, the vast majority of which comes from ticket sales. Their ticket revenue is the highest of any club in Italy, in spite of having one of the smallest arenas. Varese run their organisation from a place of passion, and have players lining up, wanting to play for them. All because of the love of the game, and the purity of the connection to history. Where else can you rub shoulders with the greatest players of European basketball, have them tweak your shot during practice, and hear stories of the famous 1973 European Cup win? Where else can you play in the same arena as these historic figures?

Passion isn't love; it's blind.

An investor is now poised to take over the club. He wants to introduce full corporate sponsorship schemes, and balance the books better. But he is a local boy, who shared secondary school classes with some of the stars. They won't let Gianfranco change the DNA of the place, or make it less human. That's not what he wants to do, anyway. He wants to make sure Varese is still on the map for another few generations. It's currently a bad business from a financial perspective, but full of love, albeit very gruff and tough. If they can get their heads around focusing on both love and financial security, and be a little

Everyday happenings

less rigid, it will be one of the top clubs in the country, and in Europe. The old players won't ever allow it to lose its sense of history, forget the traditional pre-season hill running drills, or lose the elegance of their style of play. It's so deeply engrained in the DNA of the place that you couldn't remove it even if you tried. Thankfully for Ponti, the future owner, it's easier to turn a heartfelt, but failing, business into a thriving one, than it is to turn a soulless money-making machine into an organisation that has meaning. Varese have taken the idea of 'love in business' to an extreme, but there's something to learn here. Everything doesn't have to be about passion. But money is definitely overrated, and even with a tenth of the budget, Varese hold their own against the shiny international poster stars of the Armani team. It's one of the most frustrating organisations I've ever had contact with, but it's also one of the most inspiring. It is already producing the champions of the future, and I feel honoured that my son is headed for being one of them.

Yesterday I had a call with Richard. He seems to think that he's my boss, telling me to "just keep writing", and "don't forget the other half of the story". I think he's scared that I'm heading off in some sort of 'spiritual guru' direction, and I've forgotten that I want to start a corporation, which will need products, structures, and processes. The thing is, I have a different worldview. I don't see spiritual and business as separate things, or personal and business as being separable. I simply see them as different perspectives. Let me explain. Our current culture is one in which, within seconds of getting a group of people together, cultural norms are imposed that immediately send the group down a path of 'efficiency', 'productivity', and 'outcome'.

For years, I ran a leadership development seminar called *Voice of Leadership*. Over time, I became more bold about launching people into the unknown, into places of paradox and complexity, into closer contact with reality. I eventually got to the point where I was comfortable opening the 3-day seminar with silence. Waiting. Sitting. I didn't say anything. I didn't have a flipchart. I didn't explain anything. I just waited. I created a blank space into which people would carry their expectations, concerns, fears, and into which I would invite them to offer themselves, their optimism, their whole selves. There was usually an extremely awkward 5-minute start to the programme, with people shuffling in their chairs, avoiding eye contact, nobody speaking. And then someone would say "how does this start?", or "aren't you going to tell us what you want us to do?", or "I thought the course started at 9am." My response would invariably be a question. Something like "you're wanting me to create clarity for you?", "I need to decide what you should do?", or "Silence can't be part of a course?". I would simply reflect back to these leaders, as gently and genuinely as possible, the belief that might be hiding behind their words. As this continued over the first hour, the group gradually realised that I wasn't going to do anything, at least initially, other than make sure that they took ownership for their learning, for creating the kind of environment that they needed, and took responsibility for their own journey and experience of the course.

Everyday happenings

What happened next was almost always a life-changing experience, for them and for me.

The methods I was using (Socratic learning, person-centred group work, principles from encounter groups, and hard reframing) would create a group environment in which each individual could face their deepest psychological blocks, and release themselves to be the leaders that they were capable of being. In short, it removed mental roadblocks to more fully integrated functioning. In running these groups in this manner, we worked in a counter-cultural direction. We explicitly stripped out 'agenda focused', 'logic prioritising', 'we have to understand' cultural norms, and visited a completely unknown place. There was no 'norm' to hide behind, no easy answer to any question. We exposed shared and individual belief systems, and together chose what kind of environment we wanted to co-create.

Begin with a blank sheet if you want growth and change; anything else inhibits them.

Some groups wanted to spend the days walking and talking. Some wanted to engage with art in galleries. Some wanted to sit, drinking tea, sharing stories from their work. But the linking factor, the thing that all groups wanted, was to *explore*. To explore themselves, to explore relationship, to explore difference, cultural norms, communication styles, what it meant to them to be a leader, a follower, a boss, a worker. To explore unknown aspects of their behaviour, in a safe environment, where we wrote the 'rules' together as we went along. In order to undo some of the cultural conditioning, I had to start in an explicitly counter-cultural place. A place of silence, being, questioning, openness. That jolt, that change of pace, that challenge to expectations laid the work for the group to form, and for an extremely productive space to be created. At the end of the three days, the feedback was almost invariably extremely positive, expressing amazement at how much we had accomplished, how enjoyable the process had been, and how we didn't talk about goals, outcomes, or write a plan or agenda, but somehow we achieved everything that people set out to, and lots more besides. Simply by allowing a process to unfold, and trusting each other to meet each others' needs. These psychological processes have been written about, at length, by many practitioners, especially people like Carl Rogers, whose encounter groups were known for their lasting impact on how people lived their lives and ran their organisations. So I don't want to write more about the details. I do, however, want to write about that paradoxical space we can create, as humans, where we try to see the complexity of the moment in its entirety, and where we allow ourselves to simply *be*, with all of our questions and uncertainty, with our beliefs and our fears, opening ourselves to the changes which can come from simply exploring the moment.

> *Embracing paradox is the path to honing instinct;*
> *denying it creates fear.*

In many ways, this book is the Gadfly business plan. It is the beginning of a blueprint for how it is possible to integrate personal and business, efficiency and meandering, focus and openness to change. It's an experiment, a whole story, but also only a part of the story. Yes, we will need processes, and structures, and clear products and marketing, but without a clearly expressed core philosophy, a way of working, a way of thinking and being, all of the rest is wasted. We don't want to build yet another corporation. We want to build a *blueprint* for corporations that care. And that's going to have to be more human, more flowing, more personal. I won't apologise for that, no matter how inefficient or messy, or how lacking in structure anybody might find it.

Building a corporation that has care at its core is a high risk experiment. It's one that may well fail. We need to raise millions in investment to build a prototype. No institutional investor in their right mind would ever sign up to that. But there are millions of people in the world who know that the way that we do business has to be radically different. Many of them might spare a Euro, dollar, or pound or two to see what we can come up with.

If all we do is create a large failed experiment, but it's awe-inspiring in its ambition and reach, and leaves behind a sense of wonder and aspiration for the world of business, I will be satisfied. Of course, we're not aiming to fail. We want to build a solid business, one that generates healthy revenues, but does so without compromising our humanity, the health and wellbeing of our staff, clients, investors or collaborators. And we're saying that the health of our people and the planet comes before anything else. That is unknown territory, one which is every bit as scary as the first few minutes of the

Voice of Leadership programme. But I know that exploring it will be fruitful, beneficial, and will deliver extraordinary wisdom, insight, and outcomes for anyone who explores it with us.

How do I know this? Because we will be heading straight into the domain of paradox: embracing complexity, and trusting our instincts. And that combination always works. It's simply the natural order of things. And it will naturally integrate personal *and* business. Damn, I'm starting to sound like Mary. But instinct matters.

This month, I'm experiencing some financial stress. School payments due, new car needed, while still living frugally thanks to years of illness, and not having built my client pipeline back up. It hit me in the gut today, though; I had forgotten to pay a bill, and received a text message about it. It reminded me of last year, when I was still extremely ill, and unable to function at all due to violent coughing. I had to call banks to argue with customer services, for hours, about how to manage debt while unable to work. All while coughing. They, of course, offered no genuine sympathy, instead suggesting that I should shut some of my accounts to ease my financial burdens, default on payments, and allow my access to credit to be destroyed. I had to file executive complaints before I was treated with respect or dignity, and before anyone really believed the situation I was in, or took appropriate action.

For some reason, financial stress is *the* most extreme form of stress I've ever experienced. Maybe it's that the circumstances surrounding it are stressful, too, but there's something uniquely gut-churning about it. If I think about my own personal situation, the source of stress has been from being treated like I was an unworthy customer simply because I was too ill to work. I was passed to the 'hardship team', because I said I might struggle to repay debt at some point in the future, only to discover that they are actually the collections and recoveries team, who harass and stress customers until they relent and pay, or are punished via their credit score. Only after filing an executive complaint, via the CEO, did I get treated like a person, and returned to my private banking team. So, it turns out that the stress is actually from knowing that I will be judged as unworthy, a *bad* person, for being *ill*, someone who shouldn't be allowed to borrow money, or have a normal life. It's a form of shaming, and the financial system is based on it.

Our whole consumerist system and way of life is based on it—a 'moral code', written by *bankers*, which is only about whether you can make payments on time, not about integrity, honesty, willingness, patience, reasonableness, or any human virtue. Not unsurprisingly, this 'code' only serves the interests of the banks, not the customers, and ensures that whenever we are in situations of pressure or difficulty, the banks will be the first to get their pound of flesh. But of course their mottoes are 'we care', and 'helpful banking', 'putting customers first', and 'customers matter'. In reality, they only care when a formal complaint has been filed against them, and they only put customers first when it's in their best interests to do so. In any other environment, these relationships would be termed *abusive*, but for some reason they are the norm in financial services, and they continue to be the norm, no matter how many 'codes of conduct' are published and enforced.

> *We need to choose mindfully who we trust to lead, or those with greatest self-interest will lead us.*

Maybe it's time for people other than accountants to be in charge; people with more human definitions of care. This is the fundamental rot at the core of the corporate world; it is based on deeply psychologically unhealthy views of what relationship is, what people truly need, and how they should be treated. I don't know anyone who needs to be bullied, shamed, discriminated against, or anyone who needs the latest technology, car, clothes. Nobody deserves to be treated with contempt when they struggle to buy those things.

A number of years ago, I was working with a leadership team in a financial services business. I was primarily looking at their communication, and how it affected operational effectiveness. I was told about the new initiatives involving 'caring for customers', and 'doing the right thing'. I was shown the business scorecard. On the surface of it, the scorecard seemed to have a level of balance that I had never seen before: it included human aspects of customer experience, and all the right words about supporting customers, offering choice, and showing care.

To understand better how this worked in practise,

Everyday happenings

I asked to observe two individuals in the sales team: the highest performing member of staff, and the lowest. Predictably, the highest performer was an arrogant young thing who thought he could sell manure to a farmer. I sat and listened to a number of his calls, but one in particular stood out. He had a call from a man who was in financial distress. The customer was self-employed, and had lost a few contracts, and was no longer able to afford rental payments. He was being brutally honest, open, and genuine, asking if he could have an overdraft, a loan, or a way to manage the temporary income gap so that he wouldn't have to move, or default on accounts while he got his finances sorted. The 'super salesman' proceeded to analyse his whole financial situation, ignoring the 'do not lend' flashing red warning signs on the screen. He acted like he would be able to provide a loan and overdraft, took all of the details of the man's life, and fed them into the sales computer. He knew that there was no hope, but he built the customer's expectations, knowing they would be crushed by the computer's response. "I'm really sorry, the computer isn't allowing me to offer you those products... but there are some products here that may be able to save you some money". He then proceeded to scare the customer by asking about various insurances, and whether he could afford for his home to be burned down, whether he could survive his family needing to be hospitalised when they were next on holiday. The call ended with the sale of 5 products, none of which the customer actually needed. All were sold via high-pressure sales tactics: lies, manipulation, and clever psychological tricks.

There is nothing to fear in facing reality:
it's how we see what matters.

After I had regained my composure, and was able to talk without letting out the rage I was feeling, I asked the 'sales genius' where he learned his techniques. He pointed to the 'sales coach', a psychology trainer who had been working with the team for a number of months to boost their figures. "She's great. I'm on track to buy the new BMW I want at the end of the year, because of the bonus I'll get from this." I spoke to the sales coach, congratulating her on the 'achievement', and the improved numbers across the sales team. She responded by sharing with me how excited she was to help these sales people to achieve their dreams in life. One of the things she was most proud of was being able to offer the team advice on closing sales, and how to navigate the customers' psychological landscape in order to gain more leverage.

I went for a walk outside. I was shocked. This sales coach was using techniques that were developed to help people to heal from abuse, techniques that depended on a strict ethical code, with *zero* attempt to include any ethic. She was using her knowledge to enable corporate employees to abuse their clients, getting past their psychological defences in ways that only the most adept psychotherapists would usually be able to, leaving customers believing that they wanted something that they wouldn't want if they fully understood what they were signing up to. I returned to talk to her more.

Everyday happenings

"Is this method common?", I asked, hoping that she would say no. "Yes, we're rolling it out across all of our centres."

"How many sales staff will that involve?"

"I think it's about 25,000."

"Do you have any worries about the ethics of using this psychology in sales?"

"Ethics? I'm not following. What do you mean? It's good communication, getting people to buy stuff they already want; they just don't know they want it yet. Ethics have nothing to do with it." I wanted to say "no shit". I held it inside, instead asking to see the lowest performing member of the sales team.

'Low Performer' was a kind and thoughtful guy who was really uncomfortable with the things he was being asked to do. We sat and chatted for a while, and he said "I don't want to sell people things that I think aren't right for them." He had top ratings from customers, but his sales figures were bad. He was at risk of losing his job. I asked to listen to some of his calls. Soon enough, a call came in from someone in financial distress. The salesperson was honest from the start. He recommended debt advice, said that he couldn't offer advice beyond that, but he was truly sorry for the situation the customer was in. He showed empathy, compassion, patience, and kindness. After he hung up, he said "those calls are hard; I wish there was something I could do for them, but the system won't let me." I told him that I was impressed by how he handled the client, and that I thought he was a perfect example of how to treat customers in difficulty, but that he was probably in the wrong job.

I returned to the boardroom the next week, and brought the two calls with me. I presented the stories to the board, some of whom were completely shocked, and some of whom were smirking. I said that I saw an operation in which the sole focus was money; an organisation which was masquerading as a caring one, but using abusive strong-arm sales tactics, as advised by psychological practitioners. In short, they were behaving like sociopaths. The director who had hired me thanked me warmly for my insight. A few months later he, and half of his team, left the organisation to find somewhere to work that would allow them to be more ethical. His CEO had refused to accept that to change the culture, they would have to accept lower revenues; he wanted a new summerhouse in Italy for his wife, and would lose his bonus if he lowered revenues for that quarter. The sales coach would say "There's nothing wrong with wanting what you want." I would add "…as long as you pay attention to *how* you're getting it, and the *impact* that has in the world."

We have built our consumerist world in such a way that it rewards sociopath style behaviours. Uncaring, unempathic, irresponsible behaviours have become normalised. Corporations are structured to take advantage of this, and don't have internal controls or ethical brakes strong enough to counter it. Politics seems to be following. Reliable analyses suggest that around twenty percent of CEOs are sociopaths. That's one in five corporations being led by people who lack the capacity for care. This has to change: it's actually quite easy to accomplish. All that is needed is genuine accountability, an ethical code that is enforced, and a culture that actually cares about *anything* other than money. In short, we need an ethos of care; sociopaths and narcissists usually stay away from those.

Dante is whining. He's not been outside today. I don't think I can write more without feeling like I'm a hypocrite. I'm off up the hill. Writing about accountability and care is a double-edged sword.

I'm watching *Amazing Grace*, the movie about the making of Aretha Franklin's live gospel album of the same name. It's extraordinary: a film that has been in the archives since 1972, because production errors prevented it from being put together. The director, Sydney Pollack, forgot to synchronise the cameras, so the audio and picture couldn't be aligned. The project was abandoned until someone took on the mammoth task of synchronising it all. The album was Aretha's most successful—a recording of the church music of her youth, in a church, with a Baptist minister leading on the piano, backed by a gospel choir, Hammond organ, bass and drums. I'm at the point in the movie, right after she sings *Amazing Grace*, where Aretha is crying. The choir is crying, the minister is crying, the audience is crying, the cameramen are crying. I'm crying, too.

I grew up in church communities, surrounded by music. I know that feeling of being so deeply part of a shared experience that it feels like we're all one, all part of it, all together in it. Separate and together. Moved by, and emotionally engaged in, a deeply meaningful activity, beyond words or understanding. There's something very special about a group of people who share a set of beliefs, and gather together for a purpose that's so big that they become a whole, working together for a singular aim. I miss it. It's not an experience that is very common in my life now. I'm not simply talking about shared experience, but one with its roots in *belief*, with a shared sense of *meaning*.

> *We need community, no matter how much we believe otherwise: it is how we create and build meaning.*

That's what is missing from modern organisations: deeply held beliefs. Heartfelt, meant, deeply rooted, structured, passed–on–through–generations–of–people who–believe, *beliefs*. Beliefs that add meaning to life, to work, to relationships, that help us to understand a little of our place in the universe, that provoke, cajole, and don't leave room for us to sit complacently behind our ego defences, but instead shake us up, leaving us crying together, laughing together, knowing that all we can ever be is a part of something amazing. That amazing thing is really just life. I'm not suggesting that everyone needs to have a shared belief system, or that everyone should join a church. But I am saying that without a group, a community, a place where we belong, where we share a sense of meaning, direction, and common sense of purpose, we are missing a really core part of what it is to be human. Perhaps one of the most important parts of all. Being *tribal*.

As a teenager, I learned to sing in harmony. I sat next to old men in church, and sang parts along with them. We made music together every week. It was an experience I will never forget, learning how to weave our voices together to create an amazing whole, learning to improvise a part, adding something to the whole. It has become a lifelong passion of mine, weaving and creating musical, and emotional textures. It's part of sharing my meaning with the world, inviting others to join me, to share their meaning, and together to touch the world, to leave it a place that has a little more wholeness in it. So, yet again, there's another paradox. The more we can see that we are only a part, the more whole we feel. The moment we believe we are whole, we create division, friction, separation, and tension around us. We humans need each other. We need to belong. We need shared experience. We need community. We need love. We need belief. We need a tribe. And we need to know that we aren't ever alone, even though, at some level, we couldn't be more alone in our journeys through life. More paradox.

Aretha blocked the movie from being released while she was still alive. I don't know her reasons, but I can take a guess. It's a truly vulnerable exposé of her soul, of her need for connection, for wholeness, for love. I suspect she may have felt too vulnerable at the idea of anyone seeing it, that she was actually part of a tribe, but wasn't really part of it any more, because of her celebrity. Watching her singing, and interacting with the choir, director, musicians and audience, all I am feeling is joy and warmth, and memories of what it feels to be part of a community that cares, deeply, about so many things other than money and perfection. That's what I want Gadfly to become, and what I want to see in the future of business.

Not a gospel church; but a place where people can be fully themselves, without worrying about how they will look in the movie. I think a Steinway, Hammond, bass guitar and drumkit may be necessary, to go with our gospel choir. And maybe a wolfdog, and my 1972 electric piano, too.

> *There's no such thing as perfection.*
> *As soon as we believe we have it, we destroy it.*

Standing by the pizza oven of the local *pizzeria* is one of the joys of autumn in Italy. It's early September, and as the days get shorter, the air is getting cooler. The warmth from the wood-burning oven feels good. The smell of the pizzas is overwhelming, too. *Pizzeria Tramonti* is a local family-run business, since 1904. The family that runs it, Remo, Lucia, and their daughters Maria and Marta, live above the restaurant. The girls often sit and do their homework at a table, while eating pizza. There's nothing quite like the joy of hand-made pizza, cooked in *forno a legna*. The crunch, the smell, the stretchy mozzarella. It's perfect. And the smell of the wood burning. And the warmth… primal joy.

In the last month, I've made extraordinary progress with the health of my lungs. It started while I was driving south, on the infamous 'fines from famous towns of Italy' trip. I couldn't find an old style *trattoria* like *Tramonti*, and didn't want to eat fast food, so I decided to start the five-day fast that I had been considering for a while. Fasting is a very old tradition, dating back thousands of years. It is known for the clarity it creates, for its

Everyday happenings

health giving, and for the sense of spiritual connection and purity that it leaves. I had read that it can lower inflammatory responses, and help with asthma, so I was curious. I also needed to lose some weight, as thanks to medications for my lungs, my liver is storing fat, causing problems with brain fog, concentration, and lethargy.

So I just dived in. I started with a three-day water fast. A pretty hardcore way to start; nothing but water for three days. After 24 hours, I felt like I was dying, like I was going to collapse or faint. I felt like I desperately needed food, or something bad would happen. I sat with it, meditated a bit, and realised that it was a habit, and one that my body was trying to force me to keep, out of some deep-seated fear. Day two: nausea, dizziness, exhaustion, and a desperation for sugary food. Day three, I woke up with a clarity like I haven't experienced since I was a kid. It felt like having a new body. My mind was clear, my chest cramping gone. I wasn't hungry any more, and for the first time in six years, I was able to meditate properly, without feeling like my mind was continually wandering. My back spasms, which follow from chest tightness, were gone, and the weird pains in my hips went away too. It was like a miracle cure.

At this point, I need to say that I've been a lifelong diet sceptic. I don't believe in miracle cures, and am naturally very sceptical about any claims that diet alone can change how the body operates. But on that third day, when I decided to go to a grocery store, to see if anything tempted me, I felt nausea looking at sugar, and nothing tempted me other than pickles and ham. For the next three days, I listened to my body as I slowly reintroduced food. I couldn't make myself eat white bread, sugar, or any other fast-processing carbohydrates. I later found out that they lead to glycogen being stored in the liver. I was somehow tapping into my body's natural wisdom, in a way that I never had before. It was like being freed from a prison that I hadn't realised I was in. One in which I simply ate things through habit, ignoring my instincts and the reactions of my body.

Over the last few weeks, I've explored what my body struggles with, and what helps with inflammation. I'm gradually settling on a much lower carbohydrate diet, not so dissimilar to how I ate before, but carefully monitoring the proportions of carbs in my diet. The result is stunning. Almost no coughing. Lethargy gone. I feel much healthier than I have in years.

The more I've read about the science behind inflammation, the more stunned I am by what is routinely presented to me in grocery stores. Aisle upon aisle of fast-burn, high sugar, refined carbohydrate food. Sugar has been proven to be as addictive as cocaine. Refined carbohydrates have been proven to increase heart disease risks, and to cause obesity. Yet our supermarkets push them, like drug dealers. Why? Because they sell. And people come back for more. Corporations, bound by their self-interest legal clauses, and 'duty' to shareholders, are now in charge of our diet, promoting, cajoling, nudging us all towards more and more unhealthy choices. Eating healthily is now a luxury. Studies have shown that up to 50% of the items that people leave a grocery store with are items they didn't intend to purchase. Why? Because the psychology of food is being used to coax us into

Everyday happenings

buying things we don't want or need.

Ever wonder why store layouts tend to start with fresh fruit and bread? Because they hit us with smells that leave us hungry, and more likely to impulse-buy. And what are we likely to buy when in that state? High sugar, high carb, refined foods, that give us instant energy. When overeaten, they stimulate the glycogen storage metabolism, which leads to inflammation, fat deposits, and general dis-ease.

But it's 'good business'. Large corporations profit from our lack of self discipline, using psychology to nudge us towards habits that harm us, simply for profit. The strangest thing is that we are mostly blind to this. It has become such a norm that we're no longer aware of the dopamine rush that is induced when we are being led into that place of 'need' or 'want'. It's not until we spend some time away from consumer environments, in the wilds, or fasting, that we can somehow see reality a little more clearly. While walking for a whole day to pick enough wild fruit to turn into jam, we gain a little perspective. Georges was much wiser than he knew.

I have responsibility for what I choose to eat. I'm now exercising my freedom of choice while listening more closely to my body's needs, and less to what grocery store promotions want me to buy. It's been a month since I had pizza or pasta, or anything made primarily from refined carbohydrates. My body basically can't tolerate them without inflammation returning, and my chest getting tight. I didn't used to have issues with flour products. I suspect it's a sensitivity that I developed along with general inflammation from asthma. Whatever the answer, all I know is that while I avoid eating significant amounts of fast-burn carbohydrates, my body is healthy, and the moment I eat them again, inflammation returns.

So, I'm standing waiting for Remo, the local *pizzaiolo*, to make my pizza. I expect I will pay the price, and feel ill for a few days. Some things are worth a little discomfort.

Thinking can't be separated from the context that formed it. Change our thinking, our context changes: change our context, our thinking follows.

Today, Mary and I decided to go to the Swiss mountains, in the Romansch speaking area of *Graubunden*, to pick mountain blueberries. Dante is considered a 'dangerous dog' in that canton, so he can't come without having first been screened by their local veterinary service. He would also need a Swiss public liability insurance policy against any harm he might cause. That, on top of having his passport, and rabies injections. We'll leave him at home, moping.

Switzerland is a dangerous country. When I lived there as a teenager, I routinely saw landslides, avalanches, and trees down over rail tracks, shutting down the entire valley's infrastructure. I saw rabid dogs, chickens mauled by foxes, and had friends die climbing in the mountains, riding motorbikes on narrow mountain roads, and others get seriously injured hang-gliding, skiing, hiking, and ice skating. There were many times in the mountains when I came close to having serious injuries, close to breaking my neck and back, falling off cliffs, and mangling myself around trees. The Swiss respond to these mountain related risks with regulation and control at both a federal and cantonal level. It's a requirement to fully insure your children, your bike, your dog, yourself against causing injury, or being injured. Given the risks that the Swiss routinely live with, it makes sense. The valleys are so restricted, so densely populated, so industrious, that it's very easy to step on someone else's toes, and to inadvertently harm their property or person.

Over time, the Swiss have developed a deep and complex risk management and insurance culture, with detailed management and assessment tools. They have turned insurance into an artform. They have exported this approach to risk, selling the benefits of a tightly managed 'risk-free' life to other countries, like the UK, which already had a 'large risk' insurance culture, thanks to the great fire of London in 1666. What the Swiss may not have noticed is that many other countries don't have a similar level of risk in the natural environment. The level of insurance that makes sense while living in an isolated mountain village doesn't make so much sense in an international conurbation. But fear sells. Their approach to life has spread far beyond their risk-managed valleys. The model has proven popular worldwide, with existential fears being assuaged by being 'well insured', and giant Swiss companies backing, underwriting, and betting on this trend. One of their chief exports is *fear*. And one of their biggest industries is the emotional band-aid of insurance. Where else would you expect to find the headquarters of the International Standards Organisation, or the European Organisation for Nuclear Research (CERN)? Precision. Control. Safety.

Discipline. Insurance that covers any potential negative consequences. Mountain thinking.

Small choices can have big consequences: make them mindfully, and they're easier to live with.

One of the most contentious conversations during the first day negotiations on *Voice of Leadership* was about liability. Gadfly's liability insurance only covered the physical risks which are considered to be a normal part of working life. Any workplaces which were considered 'high-risk' had to provide their own insurances for our activities. For example, additional insurance was needed if we worked on manufacturing premises or other dangerous environments. Many times, the group would choose to do activities which were outside of the bounds of our professional liability insurance, such as crossing roads, walking in public places, or sitting beside rivers.

On such occasions, instead of forcing the group to stay in the hotel, or in the venue that we used as a 'home base', we would insist that they took personal responsibility for any actions that might lead to them lacking adequate insurance cover from my company. Of course, the reality was that their company insurance would most likely cover any activity that they engaged in during working hours, but we were using the boundary as a way to spark dialogue about personal responsibility, risk, and the fear-based cultures of corporations. On some occasions, there were individuals who didn't want to take any uninsured risk. Others called their offices to check that they were insured, before taking a walk on company time. We explored this fear, opening a dialogue about culture, personal responsibility. There's no insurance that will save you from the worst consequences of being hit while crossing a road.

Every action we take, every choice we make, has consequences in our life, and beyond. It's up to us to use those choices, no matter how small they seem, to create the life that we want. If we want a life with no exploring, no risk, no fear, we're going to pay a really high emotional and spiritual price for that. Our insurance premiums are likely to be really high, too.

I chose to leave Dante at home because I don't think he would enjoy Switzerland. I don't think there's much chance of getting caught by the local vet services, or by the border guards, but dogs aren't allowed off leads, and I'm pretty sure that the locals would respond negatively if I let him run around while I'm picking blueberries, and I can't think of a way I could keep him still enough to pick berries with him on a leash.

As we get closer to the San Bernardino pass, the snow on the tops of the mountains is getting closer and closer. It's still early for snow; the first weekend in September it is really unusual to have snow as low as 2000m, but there's a solid dusting over the mountains. My heart leaps, remembering how it felt, sitting in school, age eleven, the first autumn that I lived in Switzerland. Every day, the snow got a little bit lower, and I knew that when it got below 800m, it would stick in the village, and I would get to learn to ski. I was so excited. I wasn't disappointed when it finally arrived. A local man,

Jean-Marc, taught me to ski, and soon I was going with school, skiing all around the country in some of the most amazing mountains. I still get excited at the first snow, even though it's a month or two early, and we haven't had autumn yet.

Arriving in San Bernardino, my heart sinks. The road to the pass is closed because of the snow. We have parked at the bottom, and won't get to see the high mountains, or be in the snow, without walking for hours. I will have to come back for snow. I'm on a hunt for blueberries. It's a thirty minute walk from the car park to the bushes on the lower slopes at the end of the valley.

The blueberry season usually runs until mid or late September, but this may be the last day that it's possible to gather them. We've been picking for about an hour, and only have maybe one hundred grams, not enough to make jam with. About three quarters of the berries are too soft to pick, just squashing between my fingers, so I'm having to work out which variety of bush, and which locations have the most pickable fruit, so I don't waste the whole afternoon. The most solid fruit seems to be on the north facing side, on the bushes with darker leaves, smaller fruit, and particularly those that are stubby, with roots on top of rocks. I'm updating my model as I go along, and am finding more and more pickable berries. I'm understanding why we're the only people still picking; a few weeks ago, it would have been possible to pick ten times as much for the same effort. I'm going to have to stop typing on my phone. It's only six degrees, and my fingers are going numb. Back to picking; it will warm me up.

Everyday happenings

As I am picking, I feel a growing sense of guilt. Here I am, living in Europe, one of the most prosperous areas of the world, wanting for nothing, choosing to forage for blueberries as a way to pass time at the weekend. I don't *need* to forage for food. I don't *need* blueberries. I'm picking only for the joy of picking, for the flavour, for the memories, for the reminder of the simplicity of life. I feel a sudden wave of gratitude for the luxury of living a modern consumerist life. If my life over winter depended on stocking enough food, hunting enough, collecting enough to survive the lean months, it would be a very different thing to know that this was the last foraging outing of the year. The guilt? I don't want to be ungrateful for everything past generations have created for us. The infrastructure, the methods of farming, the supply chain, the transport, the industrial world that allows me to pick berries for joy, rather than out of desperation. I feel truly grateful to be in this position.

This week I turned forty-eight. A hundred years ago, I would have already outlived the vast majority of people. The global average life expectancy in 1920 was forty-two. The last century has brought us so much progress, so many benefits, so much peace, and prosperity, and an unprecedented ease in life. Most of that progress has been accomplished through the work of giant corporations. I live in a country which now has one of the highest average life expectancies in the world, eighty-two years, against a global average of seventy-one. But this astonishing progress has come at a price. Our future is at risk. Our environment is being destroyed. Our connection to the natural world has been almost completely severed. There has to be another way, one that is *nearly* as efficient and productive, that can sustain *most* of the basic comfort of our luxurious lifestyles. We need to integrate humanness and productivity, environmental awareness and efficiency, technology and care. We need to honour our origins, honour the progress we have made as a species, and also honour the world we live in.

> *The more grateful we are for the things*
> *we have, the more easily we can see*
> *the harm we cause by having them.*

I just finished picking my last blueberries of the season. My hands are blue with juice, and my hair is messy from the biting northerly wind. My iPhone just refused to unlock using fingerprints. Typing is erratic, because my fingers are sticky. I'm off the 'allowable' map for modern consumers.

Into the psyche

I realised, while reviewing my progress, that it's been quite a while since I wrote anything directly to you, my reader. I'm not sure quite what to think of that. Am I losing my sense of you as a presence? Are you feeling neglected, and I haven't even noticed? I hope that my exploration of some of these threads of experience is leaving room for you and your thoughts about the topics. I hope that you're finding reading my thoughts stimulating and thought-provoking. I'm still passing my writing by Mary, and asking for her input. Today, while driving back from Switzerland, I asked her thoughts about the arc of what I've written so far. She said: "Your book is really affecting me. It's a very important book, and I think it's the right time for it. People in Europe, and around the world, at some level know that consumerism isn't the future. I think they feel desperate and hopeless. The idea of building a corporation together, a fiver at a time, is really inspiring, and could help people to think very differently about the future." I had to stop driving, so I could type

Into the psyche

her thoughts while I remembered them. She speaks as eloquently as she writes.

I'm sure you aren't having identical thoughts to Mary. You may disagree violently with her, and with me. Maybe you think that building a new kind of corporation is a waste of time and effort, or some kind of farce. Maybe you think that capitalism is doomed. Maybe you don't really think there's anything to worry about, and it will all rebalance itself naturally. I'm sure that, whatever your perspective, it has value, and can help us to build a better future. I would love to be able to hear your responses in the way that I can hear Mary's and Richard's. I've just sent the current draft to a couple of other people—Pavel, Matteo, and Stéphanie—to ask for their feedback. I'll have the perspectives of a therapist, writer, ex-CEO, executive coach, business psychologist, brand strategist, and journalist. I need some wider and deeper dialogues so that I can refine the narrative further.

Maybe you have suggestions? By the time you're reading this, I won't be able to incorporate any suggestions that you have into this book, but I'm sure we will be able to hear them in other ways. I look forward to that, to being able to incorporate your thoughts, your concerns, your perspective into the work that we are starting here. But I'm actually more interested in how you are *feeling*. Are you grieving, like I am, yet feeling hope? Are you feeling optimistic, scared, determined, bored, frustrated? Are you feeling *anything*? I don't mean to intrude. I'm just curious. And genuinely interested. And I wish that this medium were somehow more interactive. It's a difficult thing, creating a sense of dialogue with an unknown person. We all know that it's not possible to have a dialogue with a book. Our minds play tricks on us, though, and sometimes it feels to me like you are real, and here, and listening to me. Perhaps it might feel to you like I am real, and here, and listening to you, too. I'd like to play with that idea a little; I think that it could be useful to both you and to me. Does that make sense?

> *We are as powerless as we are powerful;*
> *to live fully means embracing both,*
> *without disempowering others.*

Oliver Lee is an account director at CWA, a creative agency that works with large brands. I came across his writing on LinkedIn, when he posted a really thought-provoking blog post, *These 2 mindsets are destroying humanity*. He writes about the importance of taking action on global issues, instead of sitting back believing that we have no power to change the world. That, and the urgency of taking a long-term perspective. His basic point is that what is needed is a global change of mindset. That's *Gadfly* thinking. I couldn't resist.

I just spoke with him on Skype. After forty-eight minutes of meandering, existential, and deeply meaningful conversation, Oliver and I landed on a really important point: for some reason, when it comes to big issues, the average person feels powerless to act. They don't see their contribution as meaningful, making any significant difference, or leading to real change. I would argue that this is the result of classical conditioning. We've all been carefully taught by the 'masters' in the world to be good 'slaves', to obey, not question, and do our duties as diligent workers. We've been taught to not create any 'chaos', or 'disorder', to not push for change, or insist that we have any power. That kind of powerlessness, human-generated subservience, contrasts for me with the powerlessness that I have experienced over the last few years of rediscovering life in the mountains. Powerlessness in the face of nature leaves me feeling awe, wonder, and joy. It leaves me more pensive, careful, respectful, kind, patient, and caring. It leaves me feeling certain of my place: sure that I can make a small difference, like by building a dam or a cairn. Powerlessness from abusive hierarchy leaves me feeling depressed, incapable, apathetic, sad, and really doubting my capacity to make a difference in the world.

The conversation with Oliver reminded me of conversations Richard and I had last month, about Nietsche's Master and Slave moralities. Humans can be roughly divided into two groups, in terms of their values: the masters, in positions of power, and the slaves, in positions of dependency. In Nietsche's view, Masters value *nobility* above all else. As a result, they value open-mindedness, courageousness, truthfulness, trustworthiness. It is the morality of the strong-willed and capable. Being strong, powerful, and self assured are valued, and judgements of morality made based on the outcomes of actions. It's a philosophy in which the end justifies the means. Slaves, by contrast, value *service* above all else, prioritising kindness, empathy, sympathy, and compliance. It is the morality of the 'weak and downtrodden'. Slaves judge actions based on whether they have good or bad intent: it's the attitude that counts. Looking at the world through this model, corporations want us all to be slaves, downtrodden by our 'overlords', not questioning or challenging, blindly trusting Masters to do 'good', to undo the harm that they have caused in the pursuit of money, power, and influence. We are expected to trust and comply, for our own good, and for the good of society. And so the double standard goes, where directors are excused any behaviour based on their status, and consumers are expected to follow, like sheep, without question or complaint. Bankers aren't jailed for causing millions to suffer, but old people who forget to update their personal details with benefits agencies are punished and fined for 'defrauding' the public purse. How do we solve this? How do we change these mindsets? In his blog post, Oliver suggests a solution: taking a longterm view, looking far into the future. Perhaps this future will be a time when Masters have integrated a Slave mentality, and Slaves have gained a Master mentality, a time when responsibility is the norm in every leadership position, and people are held to account both for the outcomes they produce, and for their intentions.

Ironically, in our quest to give greater and greater power to the Masters, we have dragged more and more nations into this artificial philosophical split, building global empires for our global Masters. We have lost our sense of our own vulnerability as humans, lost our sense of our place in the natural world, and we are in danger of losing our sense of having any agency at all, even to dam the smallest river, or to make the smallest difference to our local environment. Thank you, Oliver: you've inspired

Into the psyche

me to go and pick up some local rubbish. I'm looking forward to our next conversation.

Now we need to make that blueberry jam, and some fresh yoghurt. With only 230 grams of blueberries to show for the five-hour trip that cost about eight Euros in fuel, it's not exactly an economic success. Can you pass me some sugar, please? Oh, sorry, I forgot, you're not really here. I'll get it myself. One second. Ooooo. Tastes amazing. Half an hour of stirring (thanks, Mary). Half a jar. Seriously. Sixteen Euros a jar. We can't sell that. But it was worth it.

It's not possible to put a price on meaning, so why do we try?

We have a pretty simple vision here at Gadfly. To build a creative corporation that values people. It sounds simple, but it's actually a pretty revolutionary thing to do. Humans have a long history of mutual abuse: building empires, killing anybody who stands in our way, raping, pillaging, conquering, enslaving, then using those slaves to build empires, walls, palaces, cities, homes and tombs. Some people call this the 'natural order'. Over time, this 'order' has changed a little. We no longer have so many acts of overt violence, but we still use the same philosophy: the powerful amass wealth, land and status, then use that power to subjugate others for the purpose of increasing their power and status. All of our institutions are built with these 'rules' at the core: our political system, economic system, legal system, banks, hospitals, schools, workplaces. Somehow, having power over people, without really being held to account for how that power is held, is a norm. Many countries have put in place watchdogs, ombudsmen, and regulators, but they usually have little to no actual power, and are run by the same people who are taking advantage of the system, for their benefit, so are stacked in the favour of the already rich and powerful. It's taboo to talk about it; the 'rich and powerful' don't like feeling their responsibilities, and we all work together to stop them from feeling bad.

As we have built more and more complex institutions to protect this hierarchy, we have had to streamline processes, minimise waste, and have reduced any time spent on anything other than building the hierarchy of power. In doing so, we have gradually eroded the space, time, and energy we put to other things: we no longer really spend time in groups, simply for the joy of being together, we don't often sing together, dance together in community, tell stories. Instead, most peoples' lives have become hunts for wealth and power. Our social gatherings have become about purchasing, competing, exhibiting our 'status', trying to fill the spiritual void we feel from running after this consumerist ideal. We are living a collective fantasy, one in which we believe that humanity can engage in continuous logarithmic growth. In this fantasy, we need to continually improve efficiency, work harder and faster, and produce more at ever lower cost, while feeding the rich and powerful ever-increasing income. Some of the 'Masters' have seen the problem, and are giving vast amounts of wealth to charity. They haven't, however, changed the ways they are producing

their wealth. They're actually making the problem worse: running systems that treat people as tools, and then trying to fix the problems this creates by giving away the money they're making from their 'Slaves'. That's like slave owners giving charity money to the villages they stole their slaves from in the first place, while continuing to steal slaves. It makes no sense.

There's a very simple answer to this systemic problem. We need to value people. Really value them. We need to build companies, institutions, and systems that reflect that valuing. That's another taboo. It's not efficient to care. It doesn't build power, or wealth. It builds relationship. It builds community. And relationships are messy, dirty, and hard to control. And community breeds resistance to consumerist bulldozing. So instead, we talk a lot about 'relationships' and 'community', and continue to feed the accelerating dopamine-fuelled consumerist frenzy. We are destroying community, relationship, and care.

The simplest things are the most radical:
valuing people is a revolutionary act.

I might sound like a communist. I'm not. I'm a strong free market capitalist. I am, however, strongly anti-consumerist. It's only in the last 10 years, since the Crash, that I've allowed myself to hold the full nuance of my beliefs. I believe in market freedom. I believe that capital is needed to allow investment, building and growth. I believe that freedom needs to be explicitly counterbalanced by responsibilities towards communities, context, and the environment. Until about ten years ago, I agreed with

Into the psyche

most people who worked in large businesses. I labelled those responsibilities as 'externalities', and ignored them. My view changed while working with leaders in global banks, as the financial system came close to collapse. I saw the extent of the inequities on which our society is built, and the lack of deep-seated ethical practices at the heart of our institutions.

In my lifetime, I have watched the world turn into a feeding ground for corporations and their investors. In the last 30 years, I've seen local bakeries, local fishmongers, local cinemas, local restaurants go out of business. Their services were still needed or valued, but corporate chains undercut them in price, convenience, and efficiency. At the same time, those corporations ensured that their workers have less freedom, less free time, and less money, thus fuelling the need for more convenience and lower cost. I've watched local communities decimated by the placement of a single supermarket, leading to the loss of places to talk, places to sit, places to commune. Cultural changes follow: social isolation, lack of belonging, and lack of community. I've watched villages become commuter zones, with schools being closed, and services centralised, as local government has adopted the same 'growth and efficiency is everything' mantra.

Over the years, I've had a unique perspective on the unfolding of this global community catastrophe. I have been working as a coach and leadership consultant to directors of some of the most powerful corporations in the world, supporting them as they made decisions that affected hundreds of thousands of their people, and millions of customers. I was struck by their detachment from it all. Evaluating the efficiency of growing a business in a certain location, compared to a possible new location, seems like a very reasonable thing to do. There's nothing wrong with moving 15,000 jobs to a different area of the world, prioritising the growth of the company, and its long-term capacity to hire. Nothing wrong, until you start thinking about the thousands of workers' children in local schools, the impact of thousands of redundancies on the local psyche, the environmental impact of abandoned buildings, the emotional cost to communities of the mass upheaval. I've sat in board meetings where such concerns were raised, only to hear over and over again the mantra "it's not personal; it's just business". Somehow, inexplicably, people have taken exactly the wrong message from *The Godfather*.

We often notice what is important in life only after losing it; better to cultivate our awareness of what we value, and use it to guide our choices.

What is 'just business' to a corporate director is the very personal future of a town, an area of the country, the future of the local junior football team, of local farmers, the future of ways of life that have been handed down through generations. But far away, in the city boardroom, such issues are small, insignificant, and 'just personal', so can easily be ignored, erased, deleted. Growth is everything. Money is God. Ultimately, that means that 'personal' is of no consequence.

The more I saw of this philosophy, so rational on

Into the psyche

the surface, but so deeply poisonous in its relational, community and spiritual effects, the more determined I became to do something about it. I influenced individual leaders in large organisations to look openly and honestly at their impact in the world. Many ended up leaving, burned out by any attempt they made to change the system. I worked with leadership teams, many of which ended up frustrated and angry, unable to change anything of significance in the system. I worked with activists, most of whom are stuck in their rage against the system, unable to engage in meaningful dialogue. I worked with groups of companies, trying to reinvent their sectors, redefining business relationships. Most attempts failed, hitting a collective wall of 'it's just business'. I came to the conclusion that the only way to influence anything is to do it myself; to *show* it can be done.

We can create a business that isn't just business, where people truly matter, where relationships are real, money isn't valued more than people, and where hierarchy has its proper place, as a means of making decisions in accordance with whatever priorities are set. This philosophy has to be written into the foundations, the memorandum and articles of incorporation, the legal basis of the organisation and its shares. Many would call this folly. I'm ok with that. They can call it whatever they want. I call it 'the only solution'.

The new *human business* will be slow to grow. It won't make enough money to attract investors who want big returns. It will break rules, both explicit and implicit. It will run into legal challenges, ethical challenges, philosophical challenges. It will be a community and a business, based in a simple spiritual principle: people matter more than money. We will have to rewrite what it means to be a corporation, how contracts work, how investor relationships are handled, how legal issues are dealt with, how we hire and fire people, how we build relationships with customers, how we manage conflict. It will all have to be different. We are rewriting what it is to be a business. This book is the beginning. Business is *personal*, and we're not willing to pretend that it isn't, simply to make decision-making easier. It won't be a soft, ineffectual business like many social enterprises: we still aspire to large scale growth, high revenue, having influence at scale, to be efficient, purposeful, and driven. We're simply not willing to throw our humanity out of the window in order to do that.

This *human business* will have to be deeply creative, in all that we do. Creativity thrives where there is trust, deep relationship, and where imperfection and messiness are allowed. It is one of the most deeply human attributes. It thrives in the space between people, and is a fundamentally relational thing. It's about flex, flow, emergence, aliveness, and can't be fit neatly into a Gantt chart, a project plan, or a workflow. It's not easily captured in a process map, or a strategic plan, and doesn't obey the rules of linear, Cartesian thinking. We have, inadvertently, built systems that stifle and reduce creativity, that stifle and reduce humanness, and leave people as no more than assets, parts of a production line, cogs in a machine. We need to build organisations and systems that integrate our amazing capacities for innovation, creativity and relationality with our capacity to deliver, control, and perfect. Our system is psychologically split, and needs to be healed. The beginning of that healing is to build organisations where relationship really matters. Gadfly has a vision. To build this human business. A creative corporation, that values people, and relationship, and to share what we learn with the world. We need your help. We need your support. We need your involvement.

*The closer we can live to reality,
the less pain we store away for the future.*

This week, we've been thinking about business cards, branding, creative process, and how we think Gadfly needs to develop. The more we've talked about it, the more we've realise that analogue is an essential part of our work, because our work is all about paradox. The world is analogue. It's messy, imperfect, and over time, anything we make will degrade. It doesn't consist of binary, black and white, on and off, no matter how much we want it to. The digital world, which is an amazing way of modelling reality, is limited. It consists entirely of bits, signals that are on or off. 1 or 0. Digital is amazing for exactly that reason: we can make literally perfect copies of digital objects, with no loss, no change, none of the natural process of entropy, decay, loss. Of course, there's a limit. Physics isn't very kind. There's always a price to pay. In this case, the price is that we need to put extra energy into the system to make those perfect copies, and the hard disks that those perfect objects are contained on are actually analogue objects, so they can degrade, corrupt, and die. But while our disks last, while our backups aren't corrupted, and our servers don't crash, we can have the illusion of perfection, and make endless copies of virtual objects with virtually no cost.

But here's the issue. No matter what sort of digital object you make, it eventually has to interface with the real world. It has to, at some point, have an analogue counterpoint, a real embodiment, because *the world is analogue.* We can design all the perfect websites, perfect art, perfect objects, and perfect products we want, but at some point they will have to exist in the real world in some form, whether on a screen, printed, laser cut, or manufactured. The digital 'world' offers us a promise of things which can't ever exist: perfect objects that can be copied perfectly, never grow old, and have no imperfections. We are at risk of losing ourselves inside that fantasy, if we start confusing it with the real world.

Life is analogue. The world is analogue. Humans are analogue. Anything that we make will be imperfect, and will decay. If we imagine this not to be the case, then we are foolishly building fragile objects, fragile systems, and fragile people, who aren't capable of dealing with the existential realities of life. So, the more digital our life becomes, the more careful we need to be to remember that digital isn't real, that it is simply a representation, an abstraction, an over-simplified model of reality. If we don't remember this, our digital house of cards will collapse. Like the financial crash, the analogue reality of life will suddenly assert its presence. That's the paradox. The more we believe the myth of digital, the more likely it is that its 'perfection' becomes the very imperfection that we are running away from.

Into the psyche

Where were you, reader, when the World Trade Center collapsed? Where were you when the financial crash happened? Where are you now, as you read this? What will you do in this moment where you have an opportunity to allow your world to pause, to see things a little differently, to see beyond the destruction and chaos in the world, to something a little more beautiful, inspiring, and calm. Maybe you feel like closing your eyes, to imagine the future that you want to create. Maybe you want to stop and feel the joy of being able to breathe, the sheer exhilaration of being alive, in this moment, a moment that can't ever happen again.

I feel honoured that you have chosen to share this moment in some way with me, reading these words, allowing them to affect you in some way, however simply, however deeply. I hope that you can feel the joy that I'm talking about. It's the elation I felt when I poured the jam into the jar, the delight of the first snow, the prickling cold of the north wind on my face while picking berries, the warmth of the memories of walking through the woods with Georges as a child, learning the ways of the forest, the ways of the land.

*Creating beauty for its own sake matters:
it helps us to feel more alive.*

Being alive, really alive, is such a simple thing. We don't need any technology to feel it. We don't need money for it. We only need to allow it, like a river, flowing through us, that we can't stop. All we can do is to choose to notice it, or to ignore it. And sometimes we can build a little dam to reroute the flow, build a pile of rocks, and sit back and simply enjoy a moment of contemplating the meaning of it all.

When I close my eyes and think about Gadfly in the future, I see people doing creative things together. I see clients cooking with us at a retreat on a Mediterranean island, or picking blueberries in the mountains. I see people who understand each other, who have real relationships, talking about projects, buildings they want to build, products they want to make, how they want to transform their companies into creative powerhouses. I see people supporting each other, a community of caring, connected individuals, creating breathtaking objects and experiences together. I see music evenings, with people gathered around a piano, that lead to 'live at Gadfly' albums, time with clients that leads to writing books together, making movies, composing music. I see our personal stories, our clients' stories turning into artwork, products, objects.

I see *relational capital* being turned into *creative capital*. I see companies flourishing with a different kind of energy, a different kind of productivity, a different kind of working. What is Gadfly to me? A group of dedicated people who want to offer the world a gift: a reminder of what it means to be human, to be alive, and expressing that through our consulting, our company, our products, our creative output, but mostly through our own sense of what it is to be alive. Of course, that essence will need to be packaged and sold, and turned into products: brand revitalisation, corporate culture and leadership transformation, creative consultancy, board development, company turnaround. For now, we need to light the fire, and put the right conditions in place for it to burn. We need to define those conditions so clearly, that they can easily be passed on.

A central part of our vision is a brand called "Crazy Little Goat". It was inspired by Villy, our talented in-house architect and designer. She is from the island of Lesvos, Greece, and grew up around island goats, with her grandfather and his donkey. She spent long summers on the beach overlooking the 'goat island' where he took his herd to graze. We have talked a lot about the wisdom of the land, and how it has been lost, even in remote places like Lesvos. The land that her family owns there is at risk. The topsoil is eroding from too much intensive farming. Locals have abandoned the traditional ways of the land, which no longer earn enough. The beaches are littered with lifejackets from refugee landings and abandoned boats. We want to change this. We want to build a little local company that is 100% sustainable.

The simple things in life are often the most profound. If we forget this, we forget what it is to be human.

We want to produce honey, olive oil, cheese, and other local products in the old ways. We want to hire refugees, clean the beaches, rebuild the old shepherd houses, and protect the land from further harm by caring for the olive groves, putting irrigation in place, and restoring the biodiversity of the land. We want to build a little off-grid retreat there, so that you can join us, learn from the land, from traditional methods of agriculture, and help to rebuild some of the local environment, while cooking feta cheese bread and pea stew together in a log-fired oven. We want to install a small solar power plant that will provide enough energy for the whole village, and create a range of gorgeously simple products, inspired by this simple Mediterranean life, and the people we meet along the way. It's a core part of our vision because it reminds us that *place matters*.

> *Agreement doesn't lead to harmony;*
> *notes need to clash to reveal beauty.*

Before heading for bed, I asked Mary for some brief feedback. "I feel like I'm a midwife, and it's the longest and most painful birth ever. I'm on this journey with you: I picked the blueberries with you, and I stirred the jam, and we bickered about how to remove the stems from it. And it feels like I'm some sort of guinea pig for your writing. It's not easy, and you keep writing these really emotionally hard-hitting things, late at night, asking me to read them, then asking me for feedback. It's hard. But I think it's necessary."

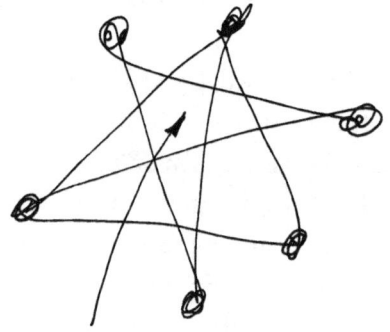

Gadfly principles

Matteo and I are sitting outside having coffee in the sun, in the *Borgo Di Mustonate*. It's a little historic hamlet, built around a stable, now an international equestrian centre. The *caffè* is in the old saddlery, overlooking the horse training centre. The clientèle: a mix of the rich and powerful, horse hands, and locals. Our conversation is punctuated by horses *whuffing*. Matteo has recently been on a *Vipassana* meditation retreat. Ten days of silence, meditation, and sensation. He has returned with an awareness of his existential angst, a weariness about working with large business, and a desire to do something more meaningful. He works as a brand strategist, and knows how to communicate what matters succinctly, directly, and with meaning. I wanted to talk to him about translating this book, and to get feedback from a different cultural perspective. I need a sense of what Italian organisations might make of the philosophical positions, the flow, the narrative arc. His advice to me was simple. Just write in English. Write from my own perspective.

Gadfly principles

If I write so clearly, so plainly, so purely and directly from my own personal experience, the translation won't matter. The book will become known, and valued, and the translations will happen. In short, "write from a place of passion". It reminds me of Richard's advice, to not care about what the reader thinks, feels, or experiences. There's wisdom in this. The more I write, the more I feel my voice becoming stronger; my confidence in my own, paradoxical, narrative is growing. But I'm still curious about what an Italian would make of it, and I value the reader. So I'm sending Matteo a copy for feedback.

Over the years, Gadfly has developed a unique way of operating. What started out as my personal philosophy has grown to become a set of basic principles of engagement by which we work. These have been shaped by thousands of hours of conversations, client work, coaching, supervision, dialogue, and experiences working with teams in high performance environments. As I have been writing this book, I've taken notes on each of the principles that I'm illustrating. I've also built a relatively complete list of our beliefs. This is the ground that we stand on, the philosophy that we espouse as we work with organisations.

These Gadfly principles are an attempt to describe our working ethos for clients, collaborators, employees and shareholders. I offer it here, as I think it's a useful filter, a useful lens through which to interpret your experience. Our principles are imperfect, contradictory, and aren't intended to be a list of rules, or a perfect guide to be adhered to; they're a set of beliefs and perspectives, some more firmly held than others, which have their uses within certain contexts. In other contexts, they may be entirely useless. As with any philosophical position, everyone who reads them will interpret them differently; they will use them differently, delete some, and add their own personal flavour and perspective, as they seek to be more authentic in their work.

Imperfection and contradiction are the essence of being human: without them, we can't be whole.

Our aim, when we apply these principles, is to create products, experiences, outcomes, companies, frameworks, installations, exhibitions, music, text, art, books, conversations, that are beautiful, ephemeral, integrated, powerful, masterful, simple, clear, elegant, existential, paradoxical, and true. We work in a liminal space, at the edge of experiencing, that takes the people we work with on a journey of discovery about themselves, their work, their companies, their purpose.

Principle one: the existential matters

We believe that the most important things to pay attention to are the things we least understand. Questions like: Why are we here? What is the purpose of life? How can we be loving yet successful? We are strongly influenced by teachings about compassion, loving, giving, and being. We balance the present moment with awareness that we won't be around forever, either as individuals or as a business. A time will come when all that we have worked for will be erased. For this reason, we always seek to look beyond. Beyond ourselves, our business, beyond outcomes, to things that have *lasting meaning*. The things that people remember for a lifetime: love, awe-inspiring experiences, and beliefs that change lives. We look beyond the surface, beyond reason, beyond logic, beyond everyday business. We don't ignore those; we look at them from a very different perspective. We look beyond the era in which we currently live, to the next, which we know nothing about. In our work, we scan horizons, look beyond the obvious, and seek deeper meaning than the superficial.

1. Stories matter more than accuracy: that's why we tell stories that are thousands of years old. The journey is as important as, if not more important than, the destination: if it isn't, what is the purpose of being alive?

2. Business is fundamentally a philosophical endeavour; if it doesn't seem that way to you, then you're likely running a moribund business.

Gadfly principles

3. Embracing complexity, and our lack of understanding of it, offers deep insight and wisdom: we have various perspectives available to us at any time.

4. Seeing all perspectives at once is the core of developing wisdom. Wisdom is a capacity which is underrated in modern society. It takes a lot of time and effort, and suffering, to develop.

5. Life includes suffering, and that's ok. Learning to tolerate unavoidable suffering is a key life skill, as is learning to avoid that which is avoidable.

6. Patience is a skill; it needs to be learned and honed, and lets us experience more of life. Carrying goals lightly is another useful skill, that can be learned.

7. Efficiency matters, but no more than anything else. Emotion matters as much as logic. The most complex problems can only be solved if we use all of our capacities together, not only some of them.

8. Instinct and analysis are equally useful and important; without either, we're missing part of the whole picture.

9. There is no truth, and that's The Truth. Paradox is just part of life. Also the whole of it. Life doesn't really exist: only our perceptions of it.

10. What if there is such a thing as a truly objective perspective? Best to keep that option open. Creating a fake sense of certainty doesn't increase trust, it actually decreases it, and leads to leader-follower relationships that aren't genuine, deep or heartfelt.

11. Don't ever forget that hope and joy are choices. Our beliefs create our reality.

Principle two: caring matters

We care about efficiency, we care about income, and we care about the future. We care about story, people, families, environment, culture, heritage, processes, and our impact in world. All of it. Not only the bits that make money. Why? Because that's what makes it worth getting up in the morning, not the spreadsheets or invoices. We value those, and see their use, but it's not why we do what we do. We do it for the thrill of exploring. Discovering the heart of an organisation, what makes the people tick, what they care about. Working out how a business can be pruned, transplanted, grafted, nourished: whatever is needed to ensure it, and it's people, thrive in the future.

12. We can't control how others experience us, or our philosophies, but we can care about how they experience them, and offer to enter into a dialogue.

13. Dialogue allows us to connect with people we wouldn't naturally connect with. It demands that we listen, as deeply as we dare, and then a little more. It is

Gadfly principles

probably the toughest martial art; it requires patience, kindness, self-discipline, care, and a meditative attitude.

14. The 'soft' side of business is the hardest part to master. There is no soft or hard; there are no sides. It's all just business, with soft and hard, emotion and analysis, woven throughout it.

15. Most businesses ignore dialogue, because it's too 'complicated', too 'messy', too 'slow'; it seems much easier to shout at people and tell them what to do. Shouting feels good, but it doesn't build genuine relationships, and there's a hidden price that is paid; employees feel devalued, unheard, and then don't share their perspectives. The people who are truly powerful in the world don't need to shout; they build strong relationships, and people listen to them.

16. There's no need to apologise for irritating people, but it's worth doing if you value your relationship with them. Provocation is a valuable tool, when used at the right time, and in an empathic way.

17. Love is probably the most powerful concept, and most misunderstood. Love is the future of business: it needs to be repeated, often. Love is an emergent phenomenon: it's not a defined place, outcome, or state. The moment it stops growing, it starts dying: like us. Showing warmth and love are aspects of being human: board members need hugs, too.

18. Conventions are useful, until they're not; it's best to focus on what's *useful*, and ignore the rest.

Principle three: rooting in nature matters

We love the natural world, and stand in awe of our place in it. Our home is a rock that's hurtling through space, surrounded by billions of stars. We love the natural order: predators, prey, brutality and tenderness somehow mixed together. It's terrifyingly beautiful. We love the wild, the places where nature is still in balance, where humans, in their desire for dominance, haven't yet destroyed the fragile balance of life. We love human ingenuity, but hate how we have laid waste to so much of the earth in seeking power and money. We love powerful rivers, waterfalls, thunderstorms, deserts; things that remind us of how insignificant we and our work are. How could we ever compare to the wonders of the natural world? One earthquake, and our cities could be destroyed. We love remembering our place in the universe: tiny specks in a vast space. For that reason, we love being outside, rooted in a sense of place, in the natural world. It is a core part of being human to care for the life around us. We strive to remember our place as *participants* in this universe, contributors, not only controllers.

19. Walking in the mountains is an amazing way to gain perspective, as is having a wolfdog. Wolves aren't scary; they are scared of things they don't understand. At some level, we're all wild: best to respect that, and learn how to live with it.

20. We're destroying the planet through our desire to avoid suffering, and through our addiction to efficiency and consumption. Part of us instinctively understands our true place in the universe: that part is awakened in contact with nature. Nature helps us to reset, somehow. Be wary of anyone who doesn't love nature; they're in denial about the nature of reality, and our core existential need for imperfection.

21. Spring water you've spent four hours hunting for tastes better than bottled water that takes seconds to find, even if it's from the same spring.

Principle four: valuing people matters

We love people. We love their randomness, their imperfection, their humanness. We love how contradictory they are, how messy, how they show care and love and fear and rage. We love that human systems are so complex, and yet so simple. Whatever their background, class, accent, history, colour, race, religion, attitude, emotional state, or education level, we see people as having intrinsic value. We try to value everybody equally, though our personal blind spots sometimes get in the way. We also recognise that there are more useful and less useful people to have in any given conversation. We think there's nothing better than working with other people, sharing ideas, mixing and matching and creating things *together*. We value directness, and don't shy away from difficult topics or conversations. We work hard to be open and honest, and to find ways to express what we see in a way that tries to avoid causing offence. Sometimes we fail.

22. We all need a tribe. Everyone needs belief and meaning, even if that belief is that we don't need belief, and the meaning is that there is no meaning. Tribes are built on shared beliefs.

23. Hierarchy is a core part of being human: it's best to channel it in ways that are constructive, and be very mindful about what sort of people we're placing at the top. Everyone has a truly unique perspective on the world. It's worth nurturing uniqueness; it's what allows each of us to add value.

24. Being genuine is a messy business, fraught with inaccuracy: do the best you can, and focus on the story that you're wanting to tell. A business where people don't feel free to cry is by definition not very human. 'Human' means imperfect and relational.

25. We grow through relationships: that's why they're valuable. Sometimes we only realise their value after they're gone. Relationship keeps giving, even after it's over: that's its real gift. If you ever go through a long period of hardship or illness, you will learn who your true friends are: they are precious; keep them close.

26. Business is always personal: anyone who tells you otherwise is probably using you. It's possible to be local and global; it's all about relationships.

Gadfly principles

Principle five: nurturing ourselves matters

We won't ask you to do anything we aren't willing to do ourselves, or show vulnerability we're not willing to show. We are constantly finding ways to stretch ourselves, to grow our creative integrity. We want to find the most effective path to get to a future that we can all be proud of. We are starting by caring about our story, environment, culture, heritage, processes. We've honed them through years of hard work, digging deep into the soil, understanding the consequences of our actions, and aiming to leave the world a slightly healthier place than we found it. We believe that healthy collaborative relationships are the fundamental building blocks for emotionally and spiritually healthy people and organisations. Our focus is the common good, and we make money along the way, developing and sharing tools to help large organisations to become more conscious in their work.

27. Being perceived as slightly crazy is the sign that you're healthy and normal. Understanding isn't something that happens all at once: it's a gradual process of unfurling of deeper and deeper layers of experience. Depth matters.

28. Everyone forgets who they are at some point in their life: the key is to make sure that we rediscover ourselves. The work of spiritual growth is a continual process of rediscovery: each time, we dig deeper.

29. Being 'successful' is overrated: lots of high profile leaders aren't actually very powerful, they're just assholes. Learn to tell the difference between power and dysfunctional behaviour; keep watch for sociopathic and narcissistic behaviours.

30. The human mind is an incredible thing; experience isn't a linear or rational phenomenon. Process and outcome aren't separable: when we try to separate them, we create an artificial sense of our capacity to control life.

Principle six: working creatively matters

Our work is experimental. We are curious, and value exploring, growth, and learning. We'll try different things, and do what works. We love learning with our clients, and we are very ambitious, so we're constantly developing new and custom methods. We'll share our tools, models, the way we operate, our heart, and we'll plan a path for our clients; customising everything for them, to transform them into the business they've always dreamt of being. We work in the moment: whatever emotion or situation arises, we work with it. We want people who work with us to remember what it is to feel *alive*. We value tenderness, hugging, and encouragement, and offer them as much as we can.

31. Exploring is a core part of being human, one that we've almost eradicated in industrial societies. What we don't know is usually more important than what we do. Exploring takes energy, time, and effort, but is worth it.

Gadfly principles

32. The number Seventy-three is the number of perfection. Don't ask why. Just accept it; I'm an expert in seventy-three. Don't trust experts.

33. Creating is a spiritual and existential act: it's about engaging with the moment, and involves destruction. Business is a fundamentally creative act: creating products, services, wealth, meaning. Ignoring the creativity of business will lead to boredom. Any business which isn't growing spiritually is dying.

34. Metaphor is a very powerful way to communicate beyond what we know. Meandering is useful, as useful as direct goal-setting: it helps us to find new areas of growth.

35. Brands and organisations which are real, based on genuine passion, care, and personal emotions and relationships, are of greater lasting value. Real brands can't be copied; they can only be imitated, because they have a uniquely human DNA behind them: a combination of relational and creative capital. Brands can't be genuine without a strongly held philosophy.

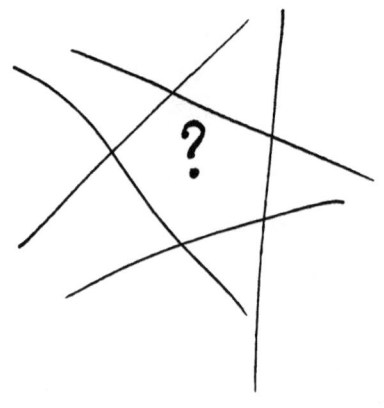

Core conditions

To grow a good yoghurt, you need to start with a quality starter culture. All it takes is a tablespoon of live yoghurt, and a few litres of milk. Warm it slowly and gently, and stop at the right point, just when the milk feels warm to the touch. Cover it, wrap it in a towel, and wait. The culture will grow, smooth and creamy, over the next three or four hours, depending on the air temperature. Too warm, and it will be tangy and bitter. Too cold, it will be sloppy and unformed. Get it right, and you've got a big pot of freshly made yoghurt that only needs to be chilled before use. Growing a company culture is identical. The seed culture needs to be balanced, and environmental conditions need to be monitored. People who are brought in, added, grafted to the group need to be carefully screened, while the culture is in a fragile state. There's no room for error. One wrong paragraph in the company Articles, and the whole thing will grow in the wrong direction. Involve the wrong people too soon, and they will pull against the delicate balance you're trying to create. Cultures are fragile things. Subtle, patient, long-term thinking is needed to avoid growing an organisation that only ever lurches from one emergency to the next, from one board meeting to another, one quarter to the next. The core conditions need to be right, and growth needs to be carefully nurtured. If a batch is spoiled, a new one has to be started, from scratch, and the old discarded. Get it right, and you have the most wonderful yoghurt.

> *Our early experiences shape us, whether we want them to or not. Best to know them well, so they don't get in the way.*

In 1978, just after I turned seven, we moved to a little village in Surrey called East Horsley. It's in the middle of stockbroker belt, an easy commute to the City of London. I was excited because we lived near the Porsche and Ferrari showrooms. My dad was the minister of the local evangelical church, which met in a converted flint barn. I tried to sit near the fossils in the walls, so I had something to look at during sermons. The barn had once housed the Bluebird, the world speed record holding car.

I enjoyed being the minister's son: I got lots of attention, everyone knew me, I was invited to all of the parties, and was at the centre of the community. It was extrovert heaven. There were three elders. Mr Quaintance ran a printing company, and gave me little spiral-bound notebooks made from leftover paper. He told me stories from when he flew Lancaster bombers during the war, and gave me his leader parachute. I tied it to the back of my bike, so I could watch it billowing behind me as

I pedalled. Mr Quintance drove an old Morris Minor—with orange indicators on sticks that flap up and down. I liked his car, but I liked David Ide's cars better. He drove a Bentley on Sundays, because he didn't want to show off. That's what he told me. But I liked it better when he came for prayer meetings, and drove his Rolls Royce. Best of all was when I went to his house, and drove his tanks and armoured cars, and sat in his jet. I liked sitting in the cockpit best, and seeing around the hangar full of planes. David had a first name, and I liked that, too. I thought that Mr Q, as everyone called him, probably had a first name like Horatio. Mr Williams was different. He had a battered up ugly brown car. I stood in the back garden of our house, and waved to him when he flew over our house in *Concorde* to go to meetings in New York. He sent me postcards from all around the world, and brought me money from lots of different countries for my coin collection. He was an important person in a big company in London. He talked a lot about taking care of people, and his daughter, Helen, was a missionary nurse in Zambia. He had lots of money, but mostly gave it away. David had lots of money, too, and had a lot of fun with it. My parents didn't like him so much. I liked him, and liked having fun with him. Especially playing in the tanks, and pointing the search lights. Oh, and the motorbike collection. And the jet. And his daughter's butterfly collection. I liked her. I think she liked me, too. I used to wonder why adults had to choose between having fun or being kind. David was more fun to be around than Mr Williams. Mr Williams always talked about serious stuff. I didn't really understand why

Core conditions

someone would choose to always be serious. I decided that when I grew up, I wanted to work in big companies like they did, make lots of money, have fun, care for people, and talk about serious stuff when I had to. I imagined flying around the world on *Concorde*, meeting interesting people, and working with big companies on how they care for their people.

Thirty years later, when I was regularly working in the boardrooms of global corporations, with FTSE100 CEOs like David, and chairmen like Mr Williams, I discovered that very few boards think about their organisation as having any interest in, or capacity, to care. They don't even think about serious stuff, like environmental, emotional, and spiritual sustainability, and they don't have much fun. Almost all they talk about is *money*. It's no surprise; it's written into the Articles of Association. Directors have to talk about money all the time, because that's the core condition of their company's formation. A batch of yoghurt made from a sour starter.

When I was five, I lived in a big house by a church, in Dundrum, Ireland. The village was on the sea, and I spent whole afternoons running on the beach. We had maid's quarters that were closed off, full of mice and cobwebs. At least that's what my mum told me, when I wanted to go in. I have vague memories of the flagstone floor in the kitchen, orange and purple curtains, a shag rug, and fibre optic light. It was the 70s. We lived at the bottom of a field with a horse in it, near a hill with a medieval castle, where I played trolls with my sister. She always made me be the troll. I watched from the castle tower as ships came into the harbour in the bay. I went to watch the coal being unloaded in the dock, and to see Mrs Hazard in her haberdashery shop, where I played with the rolls of brown paper and string. I skied down the sand dunes down by the beach, imagining I was in Switzerland. By the pond, there was an old road roller. I used to sit on it and imagine I was driving a train. For a moment I was powerful: in control of my destiny, a grown-up, pulling on levers. Trains became a metaphor.

> *Our childhood dreams matter:*
> *more than we want them to.*

On my 8th birthday, after moving to England, my parents took me to the Bluebell Railway. It was an incredible experience, smelling the smoke and the lurching of the steam train. After riding in the carriage, I went up to speak to the driver. He was a stereotypical steam engine driver: peaked cap, oil-spattered face, waxed moustache. He clearly loved what he was doing, and wanted to share the joy of trains. I asked if I could drive. He said yes. I got in the cab with him, shovelled coal, felt the heat on my face, and helped him to drive the train from one end of the platform to the other. It changed my life. I walked away feeling taller, knowing I could ask for what I wanted, and knowing that sometimes magical things happen: dreams can come true.

Almost thirty years later, I was working with an executive called Marc. We'd arranged to spend a day near Gatwick airport, to walk and talk, and work on his development. I gave him a map, drew a circle on it, and asked him to choose a first location. He chose the Bluebell Railway. I challenged him to see if he could get to drive the train. He thought that was a very cool idea, and fit well with the things he was working on (influence, communication, enthusiasm). It was a surreal experience for me, returning after so long. The tiny station, the smells and sounds, exactly as they had been. It was the same driver! After some deliberation, Marc approached him and asked if he could drive. Clive looked really depressed. He was slumping, and was emotionally closed. This was not the man I remembered. "No. Nobody gets to drive but me". I asked why that was. He told the story. Five years before, a woman had driven the train. She was wearing a sun dress, and a spark had jumped out of the furnace. Her dress got a little burn hole in it, and was covered in coal dust. She complained, and Clive was reprimanded by the company directors. He was told to buy her a new dress, out of his salary, and to never allow anyone in the cab, for health and safety reasons. "For 40 years, I've been driving trains here. I've always done it for the joy, for that moment where I see someone's childhood dream come to life. Now I just drive the train." His eyes teared up as I thanked him for the opportunity he gave me as a child.

As teenagers, we think we can fly:
we can't, but the feeling is useful.

Summer 1990. I'm running down a scree in the Alps. Barely time to think. Breathing heavily. Pounding heart. Hoping I don't slip and hit a rock. Enjoying the feeling of liberation. Skiing on rocks. Freedom.

*Power and status come with responsibility.
If we ignore it, we cause harm.*

Last year, I visited London for a few days, to see how my lungs would hold up to some travel, and to have some meetings. The trip was a complete failure. I ended up cancelling meetings because I was struggling, and had to arrange a doctor's appointment to get medication. While waiting for a bus in the evening, I felt someone scanning me. You know, that feeling when someone is checking whether you're safe to be close to or not. A guy started singing a music theatre song, trying to get my attention. I smiled. It was bizarre. He turned to me, and said "do you mind accompanying my friend home?". We chatted for a while, and I discovered that he and his friend, Rachel, run a theatre company together, and she was scared of taking a bus on her own. He had agreed to find someone to accompany her. On the bus, Rachel and I talked about performing, illness, money woes, and the importance of human connection. She suddenly turned to me and said, "Martyn, please don't ever forget how privileged you are. No matter how hard your circumstances at the moment, you have resources. You have contacts. You have led an amazingly privileged life, and as a result, you have a resilience that most people simply don't have. Please use your power, your influence, your capabilities, and your privilege to change the world. Don't run away from the challenge." Her words stuck with me. At the time, I was tempted to walk away from the corporate world, to leave everything behind. I needed to have a simpler life.

She continued, "The world needs people like you; people who see the toxic realities of the consumerist system, and who have the experience, the contacts, the knowledge, the understanding of it to be able to influence people who are in positions of power. The world needs leaders who are willing to stand up and talk openly about the destruction we are inflicting on the planet." Rachel was clearly from an activist background. Her passion, her dedication, the force of her words was enormous. And she was right. I have enormous privilege. I grew up with an amazing gift, having been schooled in the 'Master' mentality, while also being taught 'Slave' values. Servant Leadership makes natural sense to me: with great power comes great responsibility, and it lands on our shoulders whether we want to have it or not.

Switzerland, 1983. It's 7am, and I'm standing on platform 2 in the little railway station in the Jura mountains. I just turned twelve. I go to the local French-speaking secondary school. I'm wearing a new downy ski jacket. It's my first ever proper winter jacket. New school, new country, new life. The smell of wood smoke from farmhouses is mixing with the fresh morning air. The snow sparkles in the darkness as the train approaches, sparks flying from its pantograph. November. The promise of skiing. I'm excited about my new life, looking forward to learning French and German properly, and finally learning to ski. I've been dreaming about skiing for years. I wonder how I got to be here, an Irish boy from a little village by the sea, living in the Swiss mountains. For now, I am basking in the feeling of newness, my skin crackling with anticipation about the future, waiting to learn to ski. It's a magical feeling.

A few years ago, I spent three hours on Glasgow's main shopping street, with a group of people I'd never met before, offering free hugs to strangers. I hugged close to 200 people, watched as 5000 walked away grinning, and felt the contempt of three. It was one of the most amazing experiences of my life. I hugged the balloon guy, the buskers, the tramp, some grannies, mothers, goths, tourists (an American, four Italians and a French woman), rugby players, people in wheelchairs and crutches, children, pregnant women, widowers. So many individuals, all of their hugs unique. The community officers wanted to hug, but weren't allowed to.

Some really moved me. The goths were too scared to get close, but one of them broke from the pack, ran across the street and jumped on me, quivering like a bat in a trap, closely followed by the other five in quick succession, all shaking in fear. I was in tears, feeling honoured that they trusted me. The rugby players looked so surly, I almost didn't offer them a hug. I was rewarded with an amazingly tender bear hug, and "thank you so much". One woman said she'd walked up and down three times before she could muster the courage to ask for a hug. Then said "thank you, you've made my day". I felt a scarily wide range of emotions: cameraderie, fear, vulnerability, suspicion, guilt, shame, joy, sorrow, rejection, hurt, elation, acceptance, freedom, peace, love.

The whole experience got me thinking about the 'rules'. Why do we nurture this fear of contact? Who makes

Core conditions

the rules? Why do most teachers not hug their students any more? Why did most of the parents guide their kids away from us and tell them not to trust strangers? And why do couples try to control each other, saying "you don't want a hug; don't be silly". And what's up with men being scared of touching other men? Are organisations culturally biased against hugging? Do companies look down on gestures of affection? Why are we all so scared of touching? So many questions.

That afternoon on the streets of Glasgow, I saw the many ways in which people carry their fear. I ended up feeling that we really are all in it together, and we all need affection, care, warmth, love. I saw fear change to joy in seconds as people realised what a simple thing it is to show care. All it takes is making sure that you have their permission, and realising that permission isn't a tick-box, it's a conversation. Maybe it's not so difficult to change the world after all. Maybe all we need to do is care a little more. I wonder how companies would be if they ran weekly hug clinics, how care homes would be if they had hug teams, and how high streets would be if the community officers were encouraged to offer hugs. Maybe we'd all have a little more trust in each other, and not feel the need to check our pockets for phones and wallets after someone touches us.

Meeting the people of Glasgow changed me for the better. Their infectious smiles and warm hugs touched me. The experience restored some of my faith in humanity, and pushed me into a place of less fear. One lady summed it all up: "At first I thought you were harassing people for money, but then I realised you were just giving. Freely. It's sad how little that happens. I'm sad I thought that. I mean, everything seems to be about money these days. Amazing. Just amazing. You've made my day. Thank you."

We are relational beings: when we ignore that, we make life harder for ourselves.

About 12 years ago I was working in a banking contact centre. I was there to help with organisation-wide communication, and staff motivation. After a really emotionally tough coaching session with one of the leaders, we hugged each other. The staff started chattering. I wondered how long it would take to get all the way across the seven hundred workers, so I walked to the furthest corner of the building, three floors up, and waited. It took seven minutes for the news to spread, and for me to be teased for 'having a thing' with Zoe. That afternoon I was meeting with the board, who had been struggling for months to get staff to pay attention to their communication. I said "you may have heard about *The Hug*." They laughed, and said they had. I told them it takes seven minutes to get a message across seven hundred staff, when it's one they're interested in; their job as a board is to make communication interesting and human, not to punish people for not listening.

I wake up in a blind panic. The ground is slipping away under my feet, and I am falling. Thank *fuck*. Just a dream. Oh shit, I just swore. Damn. I test my feet on the ground. It takes my weight. Such a relief. Here I am,

Core conditions

age eleven, my world disintegrating. Again. Apparently we're moving to Switzerland this time. I wonder if that's why my mum has been crying for the last few months. I'm excited. There'll be snow, and sun, and mountains, and French, and yoghurt and jam and Georges. I love Georges. Well, I think that's what this feeling is called. It's scary, so I don't think about it much. Anyway, I can't wait to learn to ski. I love sledging, and snowballs, and eating snow, and… no way… I'll be going to a French speaking school. I need to learn something, quick.

Love is scary. That's why it's meaningful: it leaves us open to harm, but creates space for growth.

On 24 May 2013, a dear friend of mine died. I had known her my whole life. She was a concert pianist who lived in a small village in the hills in Switzerland. When I was little, we regularly went to visit her, and my parents grumbled about how ridiculous it was for anyone to spend so much money on a piano. I sat at her Bösendorfer concert grand, and fell in love. The beautiful wood, the sound, the power, the feel of the keys, the smell. The piano sat proud in her livingroom, filling one end of the room. It was a statement of her love, her passion for music. She played Rachmaninov for us, and told stories of concerts. Before her husband died. Before her arthritis. Her longing to play was so infectious that I caught it. I fell in love with pianos.

In my early twenties, when I was having a rough time and needed some space, I invited myself to stay with her for a while. I sat and played the piano every day, watching the autumn rain fall, wondering if I'd ever be able to play in a way that I was happy with. She used to come in, sit down, tut for a while and say I needed to work on my technique, but that I had a musician's touch. We went together to eat *Filet de Perche a la Meunière* at her favourite restaurant by *le Lac de Neuchâtel*, and to a Debussy concert in *Bienne*. I didn't ever work on my technique. I worked on my ability to feel, and to express what I feel. I worked on my relationship with my past, my relationship with my self, my ability to be in the moment, to play with love, with meaning, with joy.

Twenty years after staying with her, I bought my first grand piano. It's an old, battered 1937 Chappell. Nothing very exciting. I decided to see what I could do with it. I learned to refurbish and regulate the action, with help from my piano tuner. I taught myself to voice the hammers, and regularly played Bösendorfers, Steinways, and Faziolis in London, for comparison. I gradually managed to shift the touch of my piano so that it feels more like a concert piano than an old baby grand. It's a souped up Mini Cooper that feels a bit like a Ferrari. Refurbishing my piano changed me. I learned what it is to love, to show it, to be gentle and caring and warm, and to play in that way. I learned a lot about patience, and about the importance of being able to express myself authentically, with immediacy.

The autumn before she died, I visited Mme Abegg. She was ninety seven. She sat in her livingroom, with her daughter, while I played. It was the first time I had ever been in a room with them when they weren't arguing. They listened to me playing, looking out the window. Birds came to listen. When I finished, she said *"Ahhh... c'est magnifique, Martyn; j'espère que tu donnes des concerts"*—Magnificent, Martyn; I hope you are giving concerts. I said I was planning to, and want to record an album of piano music. Something told me that would be the last time I would see her. I had finally graduated from her tuition, even though I hadn't had any lessons. I promised myself that I would give a concert, for her. Thank you, Mme. Abegg, for teaching me how to be an artist, and that it's an ok thing to be one.

It's 1978. I'm an irritating seven year old, who wants something to do on a boring day during the summer holidays. I'm in my grandmother's farmhouse kitchen in Ireland, near the Aga stove, which keeps the room cosy in the chill of the summer sea breeze. My grandmother walks in with a dead pheasant, "Ye see, Martyn, this is what Anthony gave me today. I need to hang it. Come and help me; I can't reach the hooks on my own". She's in her 70s, and struggling to keep the farm going. The pheasants need to hang by the neck until they drop. It's how you tell that the meat is ready. I stand on a wobbly step stool to hang the pheasant, and she asks if I want to come to feed the hens. I've never fed them before. The Barn is a scary place. It's where The Cats live. Hundreds of them. Everywhere. The ones that managed to escape being drowned. The tractor fell through the floor of The Barn last year, while loading waste from the chickens. *Nobody* goes up to the hens. I wonder why she's taking me there. The steps are scary; there's no handrail, and the concrete is cracking. I hold on to the side of the building,

the raucous sound of hundreds of hens growing louder.

She opens the door. An overwhelming stench of chicken shit. I see, for the first time, where the eggs come from. Row after row after row of tiny cages, full of battery hens. They're loud, aggressive, and stare at me like they're going to kill me. Some are missing eyes, and most have no feathers on their wings. Instead, they have stumps, clots and fragments of bone. "We clip their wings so they don't hurt themselves. And their beaks, so they don't kill each other. It's for their own good." Their beaks are blunt, bleeding, warped. I rush along the aisles, throwing grain into the feeders, trying not to gag, trying not to run away. It's the most awful thing I've ever seen. I jump down the steps, and back to the kitchen, where Granny cooks me bacon and eggs. I wonder how we treat the pigs.

In 2006, I visited the international headquarters of a well known street fashion brand, in Amsterdam. I was invited, together with a group of innovation experts, to the CEO's suite on the top floor of an office building. The assistant ushered us in to a beautiful double-height room, complete with fireplace, armchairs, full length library, views over the surrounding countryside, and a grand piano. I sat down and started playing. In the professional musical environments I move in, pianos are tools to use, to play, to create, to enjoy. It's practically a reflex to check instruments out. An executive assistant approached, "Stop. It's the CEO's piano. *Nobody* is allowed to play." I stopped, but it really got me thinking.

To a musician, being in a room with a piano that can't be played is like torture. I'm an improviser, a creator, an artist. A piano is a box of paint that doesn't ever get used up: colours, tones, textures waiting to be turned into something. Every piano is unique, individual, and carries the stories of the people who have played it. The idea of having a piano as furniture makes no more sense to me than having a spade as art. My mind was racing with metaphor that I couldn't share. Is it ok for a director to be the only person with permission to play? Do offices have to be silent, except for the directors, and only after office hours? Can we create cultures where people don't feel stifled, and controlled? Most offices, most organisations, whether 'creative' or not, are production lines. Battery chicken working. I don't think chickens should be locked up, any more than I think people should be.

Gadfly will have a piano in its boardroom, that everyone is welcome to play, as long as they show care. I would be deeply concerned if they felt like they didn't have permission to play. And it would be my fault.

Play is infectious, and builds community: maybe that's why we don't do it much.

I've done a lot of performing in my life. Concerts, opera, conferences, piano sessions, workshops, speeches, recordings. The more experience I have, the more fear I feel while doing it. My whole life, I've been a natural performer; I have always loved the feeling of being centre-stage, at the heart of things. It has been a difficult journey, but I don't regret it. I have vague memories of being three or four, my dad preaching in church. I remember wiggling around, trying to get free from my mother, who was valiantly trying to stop me from interrupting the service. For a couple of seconds, I managed to escape, and ended up standing in the middle of the stage at the front of the church, looking at everyone, then dancing. I loved it. Everyone was looking at me. I felt elated, excited, *free*. I was carried out, kicking and screaming.

Age nine, I was the King Rat in a school production of the *Pied Piper of Hamlin*. I was carried on people's shoulders, singing 'I am the king of the rats', then danced a solo in the 'blue cheese blues', before dying an annoyingly attention-seeking death in the river Elbe. I loved every moment of it, and decided that when I was older, I wanted to be a proper performer. I told my parents. They said that nobody who was a good person was a performer, and that performing really doesn't matter in the grand scheme of things, because it's just a fleeting moment in time, and only about the experience. I thought, "Yes. Exactly. That's why I want to do it!" I knew better than to share my thoughts. I wanted to stay in that moment, having fun, creating stuff. I had a real challenge on my hands. From then on, I wasn't allowed to be part of drama or music clubs. I was given reasons ranging from "the music is evil" to "people moving their bodies that way, is sinful", and "inappropriate subject matter". I sat and watched school productions longingly.

When I went to the International School in Berne, we had to do big productions as part of the mandatory drama class. My parents didn't allow me to take part in the *Dracula Spectacula*, or *Homer's Odyssey*. By that point, I'd stopped listening to the reasons. I'm sure it had to do with Dracula being a sinner and Odysseus not being a

Christian. Instead, I managed to find a way to get close to the performances. I designed the sets in art class, did the lighting for the shows—a concession to not being socially excluded, thanks to a drama teacher who was willing to battle my parents. I stood in the wings, looking on with jealousy, but became more and more attention-seeking in my everyday life. I missed the Sunday technical rehearsals, but the teachers were loving and understanding; they let me decide what the ten thousand Swiss franc lighting budget would get spent on.

*Sometimes the journey matters more
than the destination.*

It was only when I left home, age eighteen, that I really started performing. I wanted to study art and music, but somehow ended up in Physics in Edinburgh. My parents didn't want me to study art or music at school. After all, 'what sort of steady job could you ever get studying *that*?!' I sang in the University Choral Society, on stage in front of 2000 people in the Usher Hall, and got completely hooked. I joined the University Opera Society, and sang in the chorus. I loved performing, especially being a pagan prophet of Baal. Most of all, I loved standing behind the soloists thinking "one day, I'll be one of them".

Four years, and hundreds of hours of singing lessons later, I found myself standing in front of 200 people in my first ever solo performance. In Italy. It was a professional gig. I was terrified. I sang my way through an hour of German *Lied*: Schubert, Schumann and Brahms. I loved every shaking knees and cold sweat moment of it, wondering if they could hear the uncertainty I felt about the words, about the meanings, but shrugged it off with the panache of a self-assured optimist. The audience was largely German-speaking, but they understood every word, and loved the concert.

Something was missing, though. There I was, twenty two years after standing in front of the congregation in church, singing my first professional solo gig, and I didn't feel like *me*. At all. I didn't move like me. I stood like a stiff Presbyterian, who couldn't enjoy the music. I listened to the recording, and I didn't *sound* like me. I sounded like a twenty five year old, trying too hard to sound like a professional classical singer. I don't think I could acknowledge it at the time, but I was gutted. All those years of work, and I wasn't doing my thing.

Another four years. Age twenty nine, I had already rejected performing as a career. I studied voice for a while in the States, with some of the top vocal coaches in the world telling me that I could take my pick of roles. I'd been offered young professional parts in opera companies without even auditioning. I'd sung in front of thousands of people, and lost my voice to stress. I couldn't see how I would fit in the classical world, and I was under too much financial stress. I quit, hunting for money. Nobody had told me that I could make thousands for each performance in Opera. I started a consultancy coaching professional singers. I worked with Lloyd Webber's artists, top flight opera and music theatre singers from around the world, and ran a clinic together with Otolaryngology surgeons, devoted to helping people find their voices. I worked in boardrooms, theatres, backstage at the opera, in conservatories, summer schools, developing a network of contacts around the world. It took me almost ten years to realise that it was *my* voice I wanted to find.

One day, at a classical summer school, I finally found it. I worked with Keel Watson, a coach who simply said: "you need *rhythm*, man". I was having trouble learning a piece of music. No matter what I tried, I couldn't remember it. It just wasn't working. He got me to pace it, in time, feeling the movement. It felt like dancing. I hadn't really danced since I was the King Rat, twenty six years earlier. Suddenly, something was released in me.

I was on the verge of auditioning for the Royal Opera House young artists programme, but completely abandoned the classical world. I just dropped it. I became interested in jazz singing, and started singing along to James Taylor songs, listening to country, bluegrass, jazz. I started playing the piano every day. I started to do things my way. Improvising, instead of purist technicality. I stripped my vocal technique back to the bone, and rebuilt it from scratch with the help of amazing coaches. I had jazz lessons, dance lessons, did loads of Tai Chi, Alexander technique, yoga, meditation. Anything to help me discover my voice.

So here I am, age forty eight, recovering from serious lung problems, and starting to write my first album of songs. I've not performed in years, but finally I'm ready; I've done the work. But now there's a massive catch. Whenever I think about standing on a stage, singing, I realise what a scary thing it is to be an artist. To put me, all of me, out there, in front of thousands of people. That's a really vulnerable place to be. But it's worth it.

Core conditions

In primary four maths, I had a teacher called Mr Jeffries. We all hated him. When boys—and it was only boys—got questions wrong, he punished them physically. One boy, at the end of lessons, always had some hair missing, or red ears from being dragged to the front of the class to be spanked. Class with Mr Jeffries was survival of the fittest. Girls, for some reason, were never physically assaulted. I expect he didn't think he could get away with it. Thankfully, I didn't ever get the physical punishment. I only ever got the cane slammed down on my desk, right beside my fingers. It was terrifying. It did it's job, though, in some sense. I didn't ever forget what he said to me. "Martyn, you can get the answers right until the cows come home, but if you don't show your working, you won't pass any tests." I can see his face, scowling, blue steely eyes, wrinkles accentuating his rage.

I didn't really learn to show my working until I was in my forties. Before then, I was too impatient, wanting to get to solutions for people, to be the one who solved the problem, and to get the credit. Now I show my working whenever possible, because it's how people can learn from my experience, and it's a way that I can have more influence, support others, and pass on my insights in ways that don't depend on me being present. I wouldn't ever thank Mr Jeffries for scaring us all into sitting still, but I will acknowledge that he had a point. I'm trying to do it, Sir. Please don't hit me.

I've spent most of the last 20 pages talking about myself. It isn't something that I enjoy doing. I hope that the stories are useful to you. I've chosen each story to carefully illustrate my own personal *core conditions*, the values which shaped me, the things which matter to me as a person, the ways in which my life has been singular in its pursuit of desires that I felt first at a very early age and stage in my development. With people, as with organisations, our core conditions of formation shape our growth. The ways in which we nurture, prune, or block that growth determines what our company becomes, and who we become as leaders. Nobody can tolerate, in the long-term, being someone that they aren't, just as humans cannot tolerate being inhuman for very long. At some level—unless we're personality disordered, sociopathic or narcissistic—we all have a deep-seated desire and need for relationship, for shared meaning, for being human and real with each other, living and working in communities of people who care about us.

> *Fear motivates, but stifles flow.*
> *Love liberates, but leaves us vulnerable.*

That process of discovery, of re-discovery, of growth and change, is a painful one. The work is hard, slow, and demands patience. Personal turnaround, as company turnaround, requires dedication, vision, persistence, deep relationship, collaboration, and a dogged desire, fuelled by the clarity of who we can become, what we can be as an organisation, in the future. It's a form of love. Self-love. Love for our stories, our past, our present, our future. Love for who we have been, who we are, and who we could be. *Together.*

Leading systemic change

Fourteen days ago, when I started writing this book, I imagined what size it would be. I wanted it to fit in a suit or coat pocket. 12x19cm was the best format available with the paper that I wanted. I tested a bunch of different books in my suit and coat jackets, and decided that the best thickness would be about 9-11mm. Using this paper, that's 160-180 pages. Writing was easy until I reached 150. I suddenly started to feel a sense of pressure to find a way to say everything that I wanted to say in the remaining pages, maximum of thirty. I had so much still to cover: my personal stories, Gadfly tools, weaving everything together at the end. Plus a foreword, index, acknowledgements. I decided to work to two hundred pages. What's an extra millimetre or two, after all. Here I am, over two hundred pages into the first draft. I have a decision to make. Artificially close down my exploration to meet the thickness limit that I set for this book, so it will feel good in the hand, and fit neatly in a pocket, or continue my exploration until it feels complete, and deal with the consequences? It may mean making the font size smaller, compromising on the margins, or having a book that doesn't fit in your pocket. The text is currently 11pt, which is easy to read, elegant, and will save some of you wearing glasses to read it. The margins are 20mm, which is enough that your thumb can fit across the edge without that irritating feeling of almost dropping the book every time you turn a page. Thickness may be the necessary compromise. Many people don't think about these things while writing or designing a book. I prefer to design all of the details as I go along, so that the experience is whole, so the words, the text size, feel in the hand, bend of the page, and the margins all add together to make for a memorable experience.

As I write this, I'm listening to Mary reading a book. I can tell from the sound of the page turning that it's uncomfortable to hold. A quick glance confirms it; the book has 453 pages. It's too thick, and the paper is heavy, too. It's a 34mm disaster of a paperback. (Yes, I just interrupted Mary's reading to measure it). It's too thick to put in a pocket or a bag. Somebody didn't think about the reader; it looks like a zero-cost adaptation of a hardcover, made for profit. I told Mary why I was measuring it: "Yes. It's too thick; that's the main reason I haven't read it till now. I've had it for years, and it wasn't ever comfortable to hold, or to take with me anywhere."

Oh the irony, reader, that I spent two pages writing about how I don't want this book to be too thick for you to carry. I just checked a few more books. My ideal maximum is 14mm, that's 221 pages, the exact number

I now have. I could tolerate it being up to 16mm thick, which gives me another thirty-four pages. That's my absolute maximum, though. Any more, and it will be that thickness where you're tempted to force it into your pocket, and it might damage your suit or coat. I don't want that for you. I would like it to be able to slip gently into your pocket: a friend that you take everywhere with you. So, I will just write. And we will have to find a way to sort the book so that it doesn't harm your jacket. *Intent and outcome.* Both matter. I'll bear in mind that it may be summer when you're reading this, and you may not have a jacket; it needs to fit inside a laptop case, a bag, and look good sitting next to your sunglasses, too.

> *Trusting process leads to wholeness,*
> *whether we believe it will or not.*

Gadfly is an experience design company. We turn every bit of what we do into art, crafting and honing the experience of the client to ensure that they can learn what they need to. Improvisation is one of the ways we do that. If we create in the moment, then it's always relevant. No design time is wasted. No long meetings to fix an agenda that ends up abandoned on the day. We have learned to trust our instincts, to follow our vision, to push for what we know is needed.

I don't know how thick this book will end up being, but I trust this process. It will be complete. It will be exactly the right size, even if it takes us weeks of editing and refining, tweaking and re-designing. We love experiences that leave people stopping in their tracks with the beauty and perfection of a shared moment. It's back to that sense of a page that's been designed for your fingers to rest on, to turn, without bouncing back, without feeling rough, without the book jumping out of your fingers.

In the course of our work, we have developed shortcuts: models and metaphors that help us while designing organisational and personal transformation. Using them, we can get more quickly to the core of the work that we need to do, so that we can unlock the behaviours needed to trigger a cascade of organisation-wide change. The models are a bit like templates. They don't remove the need for careful working in the moment, but make it easier to know where to start.

We use this seven processes model in every piece of Gadfly work. It is an advanced method, that draws from various physics, systems analysis, depth psychology, coaching and psychotherapy approaches. It isn't easy to understand, so where possible I have tried to illustrate it, and give an overview. I have tried to strike a balance between simplicity and completeness, so that you can explore the model at a depth that is relevant to you, whether you're an expert in systems change or not. The model is a map-making journey, which aims to uncover hidden beliefs and frames of reference. It digs to the core of what drives behaviour, whether individual or collective, and leads to transformational change within any system. This change affects communication, presentation, branding, team working, and client relationships. It leads to brutal insight, emotional truth, and as a result, authentic, genuine, meaningful and purposeful outcomes.

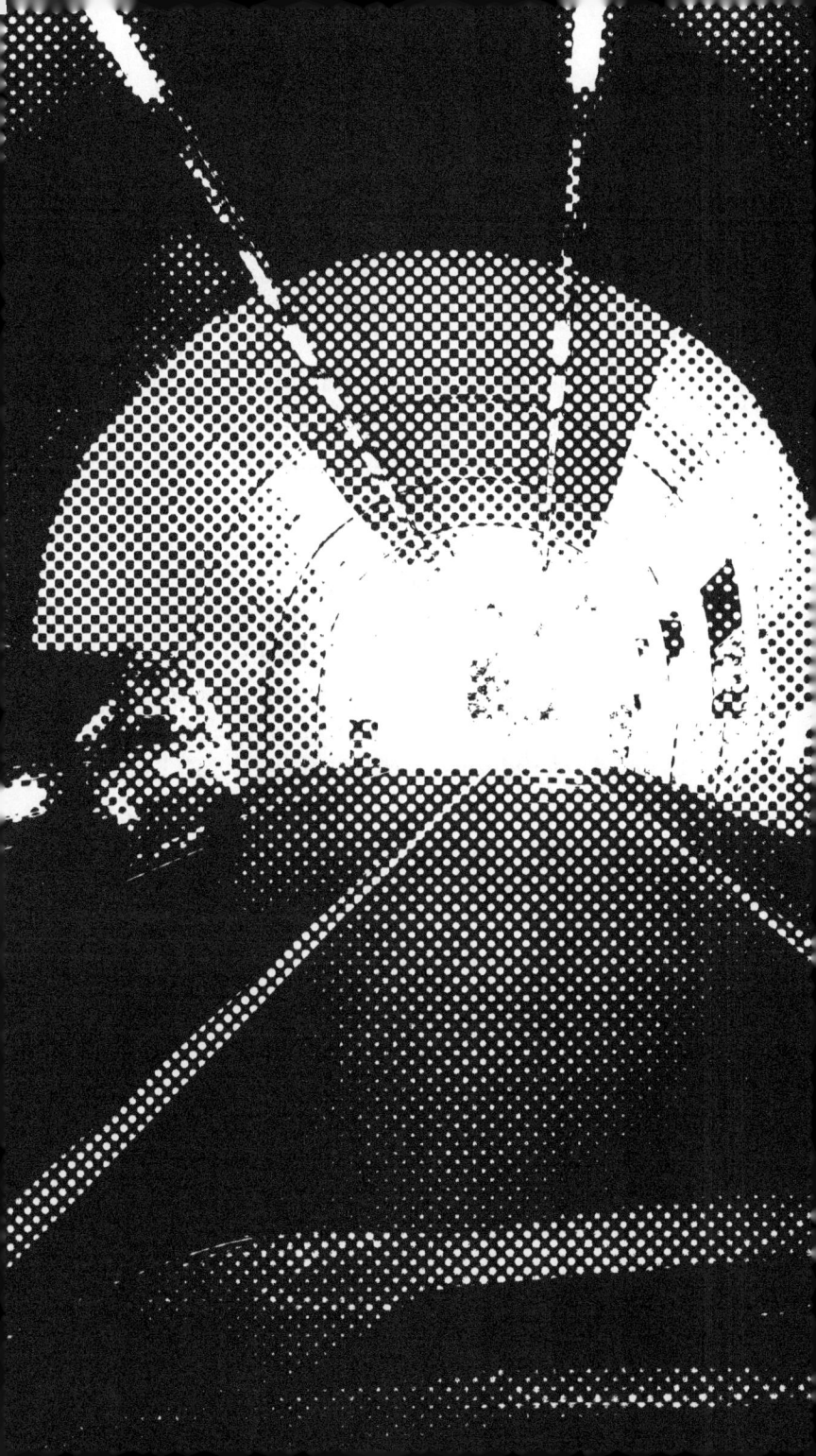

0. Create space: build relational safety.

Change is a fundamentally scary thing. We humans often don't realise how entrenched our beliefs, habits and ways of thinking are until they are challenged. When we change the 'rules' of an organisation, or change how we relate to people, one of the first things that's needed is an environment in which the fears, doubts, and 'resistance' can be openly talked about. The most effective way to create this safety is by listening, caring, and hearing people, and finding physical locations which support these activities. This safety is a really difficult thing to offer, and relies on having developed trusting relationships. It can't happen instantly. It takes time, evidence, and some exploring of what feels right, but can happen quite quickly if leaders are willing to be open, honest, and truly transparent about their intentions.

To create space for a working relationship, we look for a pattern of contact, a location, and a way of working that feels safe to the client. This sense of safety comes from many factors, including confidentiality, responding to client needs, clarifying expectations, negotiating the terms of engagement, and ensuring that we are comfortable in our roles as we begin.

My journey to find the right environment in which to write this book, to create space, was about finding emotional safety, somewhere that rang true for me, that felt like home, a place where I could easily set the core conditions in place for the rest of the writing to flow in the way that I wanted it to. I needed it to be personal, intimate, peaceful, quiet, yet wild. I didn't know that when I started, though, so I spent some time exploring how I could find my emotional safety for this particular piece of writing. It wasn't where I expected it to be, and has taken me on a deeper journey than I thought it would.

The process of writing, of creating, has involved applying these processes to my own work, testing my own philosophy, shaping, inquiring, mapping, validating and iterating until it just *fit*. I dug through hundreds of notes, scribbles, drawings, photos. I talked through fifteen years of thinking, client sessions, supervision, coaching and psychotherapy sessions. I revisited this 'space' multiple times, and have written, throughout this book, about the process of finding it, using my values as a guide. I have had to maintain a *constant* awareness of the space, checking what feels safe to disclose, gently pushing those limits, and respecting the edges beyond which I'm not willing to go. At times that has been a foreground thing, at times, hiding in the background.

Today, for example, I started to feel the need to reconnect to this 'safety' process. I was starting to get a little lost in the complexity of what I'm trying to do. I want to start to weave together all of the open threads. I know I won't do it perfectly. I know it will leave you with more questions than answers. So, I know I need to go for a long walk up the mountain today. It's about being able to find blank space, an emotional place where there's no intrusion, where I can feel clearly.

1. Explore complexity: see reality directly.

Every change happens within a context. The better we understand that context, the more change is possible. The first step in mapping is to simply explore the full complexity of what exists. This holds true of organisational or individual change. It takes practise and dedication to see a situation as it is, not as we want it to be. It involves inviting opinions from people we would usually not ask, listening to opinions we would prefer to avoid, and getting brutally direct feedback, preferably from outside of the psychological system.

Find the themes that people in your organisation don't talk about. The things people usually don't want to talk to you about, the things you avoid, the feedback that isn't being spoken. Listen really carefully, allowing yourself to be curious about the issues that you may not be seeing.

This phase often feels like it's getting more and more complex, and won't ever end. Don't try to make sense of it, just gather it. As you get further along the process, sift the information, creating categories, sorting into common threads of insight. It needs to last as long as it lasts, until you have gathered everything you can.

Typically, it doesn't really end until a project ends, but 90% of the work happens towards the beginning. The last 10% takes 90% of the effort and time, but adds the majority of the value.

Before starting to write, I gathered together hundreds of my notes, photos, stories, drawings, and note-books from client sessions. I scribbled a list of the topics I wanted to write about. I reviewed everything, so it would be in my mind, but without a fixed idea of how it might fit together, or what might be included. I allowed those decisions to be shaped by my initial exploration, by the ways that the threads started to appear. There would be no point writing a book about something that isn't real for me, in this moment of writing. That would lead to a staleness, to a 'recited' quality, rather than a freshness and genuine sense of conversational flow. It wouldn't fit my way of working, and it certainly wouldn't reflect the Gadfly way.

2. Follow strands: find the connections.

As we map the threads of insight, we need to identify specific areas that need attention. By following them, emotional patterns become clear. We discover the key elements that need to be worked on: core values, beliefs, outcomes, or negative situations that need to be faced.

Look for the tangles where these issues intersect, or a place where there is consistent avoidance. Sketch the system, then test the sketch that you've made, by asking questions about an area of experience that you haven't asked about. See if the sketch is still valid. If not, add new categories. There are usually some core beliefs that are shared throughout an organisation, system, or way of life, that link together. These are the things which lead organisations or individuals to unintentionally create outcomes that they don't want. Look particularly closely at these. Don't be afraid to ask the 'why' questions. But make sure that you're asking them out of genuine curiosity, and with an authentic desire to understand the driving principles of action.

When I found myself being really stubborn about where I needed to go to write, I followed the threads, separating strands of experience, and discovering the reasons for which I was finding it so hard to find the right place. I paid close attention to the reasons why I was wanting to write. I wanted to write from a place of genuine care, about giant issues that our global society faces. It's so easy to write about such things from a place of anger, vitriol, drama, emotional overload. So easy to miss how simple most of the solutions to our problems actually are, and how important the joy of life is.

As I discovered my own patterns, I became aware of a belief that I needed to write a detailed account of my experiences solving hugely complex, system-wide human problems, so that I could pass on that wisdom to others. I was aware of a sense of pressure to *be useful*. I was aware of wanting to influence, but not manipulate. I discovered a set of beliefs that I held about how books should be structured, what makes them useful, what good writing should be, and so on. The more I followed those threads, the more I realised that I was on a journey of discovery about myself, my work, and that sharing my journey of discovery, no matter how crazy it might seem, might be the most useful and powerful thing that I could do. Not with the intent to break convention, but with the intent to give as accurate an account as possible of what I really want to say about love, and about business.

That process of getting to know *self* is the core of therapy, the core of coaching, the core of organisational change, the core of branding, and of systems transformation. At its heart, it's about relationship, about self and other, about two entities who are willing to put effort into getting to know each other, because there's something attractive about the other. In the process, we dig into each other's worldviews, gradually seeing the other more clearly, and have the opportunity to show more acceptance, more love. Love is a process of revealing. It's a gradual, long, arduous journey, of learning to see and value difference, of seeing a person, animal, place, and seeing their positives and negatives, their strengths and their weaknesses, and valuing all of what they are, even though they cause us pain, take up energy, time, and attention.

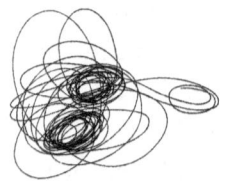

3. Map the terrain: find what matters.

The next step is to produce a detailed map of what is important to the client, and what the client avoids. Most of these points on the map won't be obvious to the organisation or individual, as they are internal object relationships. Every system, organisation, group and individual contains attraction and avoidance, values and 'anti-values'. We can model these aspects of the client's world, and test the model against reality. As it is tested and refined, their awareness shifts, and they become more able to see what of their worldview is accurate, and what isn't.

We can learn as much about a system by monitoring the things it avoids as by noting what it pays attention to. Emotional avoidance is easy to spot. If we ask a direct, focused question, and the answer isn't straightforward, there's likely to be some avoidance present in the system. Unless, of course, we're unaware of the complexities in the system, in which case we may simply be exploring our own ignorance. If one question leads to avoidance, try another. If it does too, try a different angle. Eventually, you'll end up with a very precise 'position' for the psychological object that is being avoided.

Work carefully and cautiously as you make a list of topics being avoided: there are often very strongly held beliefs involved. The aim is not to *change* the system in any way, but to simply *note* how it operates, so that you can offer insight about what is keeping it operating in the way that it currently is.

In the early stages of this book, I was writing about meandering. At the time, I was questioning myself: "Am I just writing about exploration as a way of avoiding the hard stuff? As a way to avoid tackling what love in business really means? Is all of this walking really necessary?" I came to the conclusion that I wasn't avoiding anything, but was actually in a very careful process of exploration, and needing to tease it apart, to be sure that I was genuinely exploring, and not simply avoiding writing. Richard pointed out to me, indirectly, after reading some early pages, that I may actually be so afraid of the reader being bored, or not following, that I may actually be *creating* boredom and confusion. He sent me information on 'target fixation', a phenomenon where people are so focused on avoiding a catastrophic outcome that they inadvertently *create* it. I, of course, disagreed violently, because that exploration was a deep part of my process, and needed to be thorough, careful, and in writing.

I wanted you to be in the process with me. At the time, I didn't know why, but now that I am reflecting on it, I can see that I needed to build an extended metaphor, sharing my internal journey with you, so that you could understand some of the deeper and finer points of how change works in human systems. There was no avoidance, but Richard was on the mark, as there was the potential for avoidance. If I hadn't been as aware as I am of my own inner workings, his insight would have been enormously valuable.

I expect that the meandering start to the book, while potentially irritating and confusing, will have some of the psychological impact that the first day of the *Voice of Leadership* programme had on participants. It's likely to stir some things up for you, challenge some beliefs, leave some readers reaching for their safety nets. They are likely to reach first for their core beliefs, leaving their maps of the world nearer the surface, and their avoidances more clearly present. I'm sure that there are some who will stop reading, in disgust. Our approach is unlikely to be one that would work well for them. For those of you who became aware of some of your avoidance strategies while reading, there may have been a rich reward in this book. A deep insight, awareness, or some new-found patience with people who have different views of the world.

As we seek to clarify any avoidance in a system, we also look to find the attractors: subjects that people can't stop talking about, don't ever avoid, always seem to come back to. That's where the passion, the love, the energy is in the system. To find them, try to change the topic of conversation, shake things up, ask them where they went on holiday and why. Soon you'll find that the risk managers' passion is perfect experiences, smooth operations, and they holiday in Switzerland. And you'll find that the brand director loves communication, flair, elegance, and for that reason, they holiday in Italy. Growth comes from accepting the 'avoidances' within our worldview, and from embracing our 'attractors'. The things which attract us are almost always the opposites of those which repel, just as our strengths are our weaknesses.

Organisations, as individuals, have their own unique emotional terrain. Exploring this landscape, noting the weird little 'rules', and 'terms and conditions', is a powerful way to promote change. We can discover the ways in which a business is inadvertently stifling itself, undermining its people, or imposing a set of beliefs that doesn't fit the customers it is serving. But a risk manager can't be turned into a brand manager, any more than a bank can be turned into a meat processing factory. Find the attractors and avoidances, understand the complexity of the system, and you can turn a risk manager into a CEO, and a bank into a utilities company. It's all about whether the map fits the purpose. Whether the culture fits the brand, fits the services, products, clients, staff. So, in some senses, there is no such thing as culture change; there's only discovery, revealing and enabling. In the same way, there's really no such thing as personal change. All that actually changes is our relationship with ourselves and our stories.

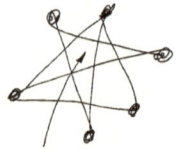

4. Create a model: simplify where possible

After mapping, we help clients to create a simplified model of their system. Our aim is to find the minimum complexity that describes most of the behaviours. During this process, we usually uncover a significant gap in their understanding of themselves. It's a bit like discovering the missing piece of a jigsaw puzzle. We test thoroughly, to check that the assessment is accurate. So, once we know the full complexity of the system, and have a sense of the attractors and avoidances, it's possible to create a simple approximate map of the psychological landscape that we're working with. Of course, we can start doing this right from the beginning, but we then need to be prepared for recreating it lots of times. Otherwise we can blind ourselves to new information, and have a fixed and rigid view that doesn't shift as the data does.

It doesn't matter if we're coaching someone, coming up with a new brand tagline, working with a board to streamline communication, or supporting multiple corporations to collaborate, the key component we need is a map of the emotional territory. In that map, the avoidances, the attractors, and the relationships between them become very obvious.

While writing, I realised that I wanted to codify a set of Gadfly principles. I had already explored much of what I wanted to write about, so I simply went through, summarising the nuggets that each paragraph was attempting to influence. I collated them, sifted them, simplified them, and framed them using an old 'ethos' statement. I simplified the list, editing paragraphs and summaries, until it just felt right. A simplest possible model that covered everything I wanted to say.

Once we have a map, as complete as it needs to be, we look for the heart of it. What is the part that holds this emotional map together? What is the question that we could ask that the system in its current state simply couldn't cope with, that would send it reeling, realising that it is avoiding 50% of its experience of the world, because of a desire to protect its rules?

In the case of the Gadfly principles, they include a deep understanding of psychological splits, and are an attempt to integrate paradoxical positions. For this reason, there is no question that I could find that would destabilise the position, other than "but what will this human-business actually do?" The question that ended up transforming my view of Gadfly. It needed to be asked at exactly the right time: once the philosophical frame had been simplified.

5. Probe the core: ask the tough questions.

So, now is the time to ask the tough questions. Time to see what the missing piece actually consists of. Is it a set of beliefs, a forgotten story, an inaccurate story? As we gently probe this core, the whole structure of the system shifts, realigning to include the missing piece. If we can find a way to gently, caringly, lovingly ask those questions, the prohibited questions, the questions that might destroy the map... if we can build enough trust, enough rapport, enough genuine and deep connection... if we have listened and heard, and shown that we see and understand the complexities of what the human system is carrying, is dealing with, and is facing... if we show love...

If, and only if, we do all of those things, can we get away with probing the core. The question usually comes in the form of 'what if...', or 'how would...' hypothetical scenarios. What if the efficiency of a bank might be better used to help the poor and needy? What if the risk management structures that you've developed could save millions of lives? What if the brand manager was no longer allergic to stasis, and the risk manager was no longer afraid? What if nationalism is simply the sentiment of groups who feel marginalised and devalued? What if migration is evidence of real and deep human suffering? What if the world as we know it has to end, and we have to put an end to consumerism? Those sorts of questions. What if Gadfly became a movement? What if the core of our work is experience design? What if building a prototype corporation could trigger whole-system change? What would this book be like if I stopped trying to be analytical?

That last question led me to removing the four page table of contents, removing grey text boxes, subsection titles, and helped me to gain the confidence to just write what I needed to write. I stopped trying to write a business book, and instead focused on the most effective way to deliver the message I wanted to communicate. Long paragraphs, labelled principles, elegant design, and a fearless embracing of process.

These 'core probing' questions are the sort that strike fear into every board of directors, that shake industries. They are usually shut down in meetings, with the questioner being removed by security. But those kinds of questions are the only way to transform a system. When we allow ourselves to ponder the questions that we're too afraid to ask ourselves, our world transforms. We suddenly have a new point of focus. A new data point gets added to our world, and the old model collapses. We can shed lots of beliefs, memories, attitudes, emotional responses, and allow new growth, new feelings, new models to grow.

For me, that happened in the most dramatic way while studying Physics at University. I had grown up in a Christian home, spent most of my life around Christian beliefs, and within the confines of the church community. I didn't consider myself to be a hardened 'believer', but when I studied quantum mechanics, Heisenberg's uncertainty theory, and some of the deeper philosophical questions that these theories leave us with, my world was shattered. At the time, I didn't have anyone with me, caring for me, showing me love while my world split open. I had a dawning realisation that nothing in the world was as I imagined it to be. I saw, in that moment, beyond the limits of the belief system that I carried, beyond the things that mattered to me, the things I wanted to avoid. I hit a wall.

If I had experienced someone like you, reader, sitting listening to me, trying to understand my world, mapping my experience, and helping me to see that I had just been exposed to questions that were larger than my current model of the world, that there was nothing to be scared of, and I simply needed a 'software update'… I could have relaxed, and enjoyed the changes. I could have let go of the old model, and allowed the new to take its place. I eventually ended up seeking a therapist, and rebuilding my views of the world one by one. I found someone who could just observe whether my model of the world was working for me or not, helping me to build one that fit better.

Companies, no matter how large or small, all end up in similar situations. The conditions in which they were founded no longer exist, and customers want something different. It's not that there's anything intrinsically wrong with the old; it's that the world has changed a bit, and the company's models are out of date. In those situations, more often than not, leaders push for more of the same. Harder, faster, stronger. Efficiency is king. Meetings clipped to minutes. Workers exhausted, burned out, sour. Unions involved, customers unhappy. Profits dive, and the organisation becomes *stagnant*. Where there was once a thriving organism, there is now almost nothing but stuckness, falling revenue, squeezed profits, complaints, high staff turnover, procedure dominating, silo thinking, a fear-based culture, with bullying on the rise, hierarchy mattering more than relationship, a lack of empathy, indirect communication, politics, change programmes, lots of tweaks but no real difference, empty social events that everyone groans about, a 'just follow the rules' mentality, fights about desk space, low levels of collaboration, honesty being avoided, measurement and reporting taking over, and customers being pressured for sales. You get the picture. It's not pretty.

6. Prune the old: change beliefs.

As the client accepts the new, more accurate model of reality, they let go of old beliefs, limitations, and behaviours. They learn to see more clearly, even in the middle of complexity. We support them to explore their new self-concept, testing it, and checking that the growth is embedded, sustainable, and fits their context. By asking *The Questions That Dare Not be Asked*, and encouraging people to think about them, we unlock change across the system, shaking loose the old beliefs, and leaving room for new, more relevant, more deeply founded beliefs. It's a bit like shedding a skin, or rebranding from the inside out. Rather than the superficial experience of change that most businesses go through while restructuring and changing their management, organisations can go through a DNA upgrade, changing their entire working philosophy, emotional map, and view of the world. They can do this while maintaining the best of the old, and having some genetic modifications to allow them to grow and develop in ways that nobody thought possible.

This book is unrecognisably different from the first full draft. It had 20 photos, fragmented paragraphs, intrusive grey boxes, and no sketches. By allowing ourselves to ask the toughest questions we had about the book, we realised that the photographs were detracting from the flow of the text, the grey boxes interrupted the arc of the book, and the sketches I had considered adding simply didn't look finished. We had to scrap the whole concept, and begin a fresh design.

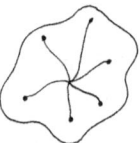

7. Nurture growth: take ownership.

The final stage involves supporting the client to take full ownership of their new model. They need to take responsibility for defending, pruning, honing, and adjusting it. It's a 'handing over' process. Nurturing growth involves creating a container for the fresh 'operating system'. That can be anything from a new company, new division, a new building, brand, to new clothing, a change of name, or simply clarity about how we want things to be. Without nurturing growth, over a significant period of time, old habits, which have been practised over years, can easily come back, swamping the new growth and preventing a different future. At this point, we gradually phase out our involvement, ensuring that the individual, group or business is continuing to grow on its own without our involvement. We sit and watch them fly.

We don't consciously use this model or these processes. But if you were to watch us working, you would be able to see all seven processes at work, held in the frame of the space. Looking at them as a linear sequence may help you to understand better, but that's not how they work. They weave in and out, always present, in different proportions, based on what's happening in the moment. But there comes a time when it just feels like the process is complete. That sense of completeness needs to be respected, or we can inadvertently stifle growth.

The beginning is about exploration, the middle is about shifting relationships, and the end is about handing over ownership. Clients have described the effect as "being taken apart into lots of pieces and put back together again in the right order". The process has the same effect on individuals, groups and businesses. It increases clarity, congruence, sharpness and definition, and leaves clients with a new and more purposeful sense of direction.

I'm worrying. Not a lot. Just a little. About what will happen when I finish writing this book. It is something I have been mulling for ten years, and has been a singular aim for the last fourteen days. I know that I'll reach the end of the writing process, and my life will feel a little empty, because I won't be able to say "I'm writing a book". I don't know how these concepts will be received. I'm getting a sense of it from the conversations I'm having, but I really won't know until the whole book is out there.

Something doesn't feel right, though. I turn my attention for a moment to the cover, the frame that will carry this book into your hands. The current cover clashes with Gadfly's philosophy of "beautiful, ephemeral, integrated, powerful, masterful, simple, clear, elegant, existential, paradoxical, and true". The design would fit in the business section, with blue sky, black buildings, and an orange dawn behind the silhouettes. It's too harsh, and the colours jar: not subtle, not paradoxical, not beautiful enough to be a Gadfly book. I decide to start from scratch with the cover, playing with colours. For a moment I imagine all of the work hasn't been done, and the cover design process hasn't been completed.

Notice subtle feelings that something isn't right: there's truth in them.

I look at the book title, "Love: The Future of Business", against a blank page, and immediately return to an early concept I had: a plain pink cover. I add the mountain back in, but this time in a subtle blue-ish purple. I play with transparency in the city skyline, fading it, but I miss the dark, deep blacks that it had. I want the mountain to be the focus, and the city to be strongly present, but somehow fading. These are important changes. No wonder I couldn't imagine the book out in the world. It had the wrong balance on the cover: the hill wasn't central enough. Now I have exactly the same design, but with radical changes in the relationship of the different elements, having reconstructed it to align it to the meaning of the book.

This process of iteration, alignment, subtly nudging towards the inside and outside meeting, is one I know well. It's the core of Gadfly's work. We try something. Set a goal. Work towards it. Explore the terrain. Notice the gaps. Adjust the target. Adjust the work. Test and refine, until it all feels right. Until it feels finished, whole, and *true*. It's a very particular kind of iterative process. We get from A to B, but by the time we get to where we thought B was, the target has shifted, and we're now heading to C, using a different style of working. Before we know it, we're at G, having accomplished more than we ever set out to, reaching further, deeper, broader, and leaving the original target far behind. That's how emotionally-aware goal setting works. It's more powerful, and faster, than the logical steps alone, but takes more patience, makes more mess, and forces flexibility, improvisation, and humanity.

A week later, after sending the final version for proofreading, I text with Richard. He mentions that the writing left him in a reflective place, and gave him a sense of wanting to join dots. He questions the title of the book, suggesting that it might be too leading, giving away too much. I remove the word 'Love' from the cover design, leaving "The Future of Business". The 'not quite right' feeling I've had for the last week goes, but now I need to redesign the cover. I start from scratch again.

For the next two days, I wrestle with the cover. I add a subtitle, "Leading for systemic change". It's now commercial, 'punchy', direct, and insightful, but looks like a 'business' book. It simply isn't *true* any more: it looks more accessible than it actually is, and more 'corporate'. I return to the original concepts: simple, pink, minimalist. I change the font to italics. It adds urgency, and a sense of something novel and different, out of the ordinary: elegant, creative, artistic. I add the word 'spiritual' to the subtitle, it now reads "Spiritual leadership and systemic change". That feels more true, but I worry about how it will be received. I decide that it doesn't matter. It is what this book is about: thinking spiritually, beyond ourselves and what we know, building ethical organisations. I remove the city skyline, leaving only the hill with the peak on the front. The hill is fighting the title, so I flip it left to right. It now looks like a downward trend graph of a collapsing system. Every element now has more meaning. But something is still missing. In the middle of this dilemma, my phone rings. I had forgotten a call.

Ailsa is an HR director who has worked for years in people and operations roles, and has a strong sense of ethic, a desire to really value people, and is driven to build companies where people are really valued. I care about her opinion. I apologise for my lack of focus, and tell her I'm in the middle of a redesign of the cover, having just taken the word love out of the title. She gasps: "but I really liked it". Her words, and how much she clearly means them, hit home. It is important. It reminds me of the words of Helena Clayton and a number of others on LinkedIn, where I posted an invitation to test-read the book. Helena has researched and written about *Leading from Love*, and suggested we might need a 'love tribe'. We discussed putting a book together to share insights from practitioners in the area. These connections matter.

But how can we find each other, or build a tribe, if love isn't in the title? How can we grow a movement if we're scared of leading people? It needs to be owned. I look at the notes I scribbled a few weeks ago: 'write the book', 'fly the flag', 'go for broke', 'what if we had a tribe of thousands?', 'what if every organisation had a champion?', 'start with those who *get* it', 'nurture the core'.

I change the title again. Back to the original, *Love Incorporated*, which I rejected two weeks ago. For some reason, after all of these iterations, and after my rich conversation with Ailsa, I realise that I actually do want to find a way to 'capture' love, and weave it throughout the legal structures of a company. That's what this book is: a beginning, a conversation about why we need to start. But now I'm left with more work. I need to add two pages to the book, re-register the title, update the index, change the page layouts, recreate the table of contents and redesign the cover. It's worth it, though. I'm just hoping it's the last piece of insight I get from a conversation. Maybe it's time to switch my phone off.

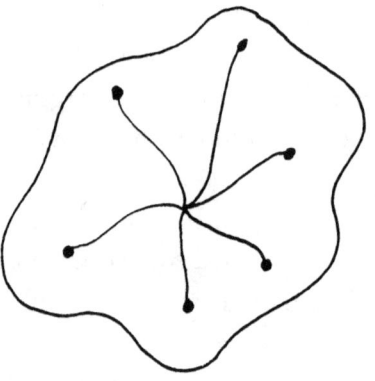

The future of business

I've pretty much said everything that I want and need to say. Nestled between my words, within the stories that I've told, there are complex layers of wisdom and meaning. But the future of business is actually quite simple. We need to find ways to see *beyond money*, to find meaning and purpose that has deep human roots. We need to find ways to have pianos in the boardroom, meetings in the forests, afternoons spent picking blueberries, singing by campfires, and making jam for clients. Of course I mean this metaphorically as well as literally. We need to make room for the imperfect, as well as for the perfect, make time for intuition as well as for analysis. We need flowing dialogue, in addition to agenda-led discussions. We need wildness, creativity, meandering, discovery, improvisation, and unapologetic exploration. We need to heal the splits that we created within ourselves so that we could sustain the unsustainable. In doing so, we will start the process of recovery that is necessary in ourselves, our teams, our companies, and societies. We need to remember that *Jam is Life*, and that time spent in nature, connecting to our environment, isn't only leisure; it's a core part of what it is to be human. To be connected, part of a tribe, learning to love: simple, instinctual, and deep.

If we don't apply our philosophy to ourselves, why would we expect anyone to listen to us?

I've just re-read the section on Gadfly's seven processes, and one sentence jumped out. "Gadfly is an experience design company." While writing that section, I had no idea I had discovered a radical new way to see what we do. We have predominantly worked with large-scale transformative change. We have coached leaders on communication, creativity, influence, impact, and effectiveness. We've run workshops and worked with teams as they went through change. We have advised boards on systemic change, supporting innovation, and using creativity as a way to encourage people to see things differently in organisations. We've worked with CEOs, CFOs, CROs, CIOs, People directors, Directors of Marketing, Branding, and Communication, Chairmen, Heads of Audit, Finance, Compliance, Change. The list goes on and on. We've worked in lots of locations: hotels, art galleries, art studios, recording studios, mansions, gardens, by rivers, on lakes, in mountains, at railways, shipyards, in a speedboat on the North Sea, in cars, tunnels, cafés, skyscrapers, and boardrooms.

On each and every occasion, in every environment, and for every assignment, we have paid extraordinary attention to the experience that people were going through. It's what leads to *change that sticks*. It's what leads to giant, unexpected outcomes. It's the thing that leaves clients awe-inspired. We have been carefully crafting experiences for seventeen years. It's our method. It's our thing. It's what we do. But it wasn't until writing this book that we have seen it with such clarity. While writing about how we work, we have applied our own principles to ourselves. The result is a mind-boggling level of clarity that we've spent years searching for. It's so obvious now. As I'm looking over the book, editing, shaping, and refining, it is clear to me that the process of writing has been a transformational experience, both for me and for Gadfly. The strangest part is that this is the last bit of main text that I'm writing. It's day sixteen. After the end of the book. After the postlude, after Verzasca, after the final edit. This chapter simply didn't feel right. It just didn't fit. It started off as a piece of slightly abstract writing about love and business, and it didn't feel right after editing "A new model", and seeing the words "Gadfly is an experience design company". I'm baffled by how it's possible for us to have missed this level of clarity about the core of our work.

Gadfly clearly needs a business plan that focuses on transformational experiences. I've always thought of us as a kind of 'personal trainer' to corporations; we create a space in which transformation can happen. But designing experiences, so that other organisations can provide them, is a whole new level of complexity, difficulty, and challenge. It will take me some time to get my head around it. That's what is at the heart of creating a corporation that cares; a prototype that allows us to experience what a new style of corporation might be like. It is an experience which will be transformational. It will be unlike anything we've come across; a giant experiment, tackling some of the biggest issues that we are facing as a society, starting by transforming the way that business operates.

Faith

When facing the need for wholesale change, we need to believe that our actions can make a difference. We need to have confidence in our beliefs; we need faith. We need to take urgent action to deal with the major issues in the world: poverty, displaced people, political unrest, social collapse, ageing populations, discrimination, shocking inequality, poisoned oceans, global warming, pollution, and spiritual unease. No matter how small or meaningless we feel like our contribution is, we need to believe that it matters. We can't tell what the future holds: whether it will hold mass destruction, famine, flooding, discontent, and failing crops, or whether we will be able to solve these issues through technology, careful management, and being more generous with redistribution of wealth. We don't know. But what we do know is that taking action matters. Even small changes to our thinking, to how our organisations are structured, to the ways that we do business, can have enormous knock-on effects.

It reminds me of working with an executive, a number of years ago, whose main aim was to have four million pounds in the bank by the time he was forty. He wanted to have freedom and time to spend with his family. He was working fourteen hour days to get this freedom. When I worked with him, flying to London for the day, I used to simply say that I needed to leave by 4pm, because I didn't want to miss reading good night stories to my kids. I was worried I would have my contract cancelled, no future work. Instead, he spoke to me about it. He thought I was really brave, putting my family first. I asked him why he didn't. He said he was, but in a different way. I asked what age his kids would be by the time he had the money to stop working. Sixteen and eighteen. I said "and you think they will want to spend time around you when they're that age, if you don't spend time around them now?". The next week, he tried eight-hour working days, and didn't ever switch back. Small things. Meaningful things. But with long-term consequences. Stick to your beliefs. Have faith.

Hope

Six years ago, when my asthma was at its worst, my body was wracked with pain, my liver struggling, and my joints were inflamed. I was referred to physiotherapy. In the first session, the physio said to me "You're forty-two; you can't expect to be able to do things you could when you were younger." I replied by pointing out that a year before, I had no problems with any of the activities, and my body was simply struggling. She continued to act like I simply needed to accept my lot, and not ever hope for recovery. I asked for a new physio. The next physiotherapist said "in your condition, at your age, you may never be able to walk pain-free". I simply said that I wasn't interested in focusing on what I may or may not be able to do; I was interested in building my capacity, and if he wasn't willing to help me, I would just find someone who could. I didn't ever give up hope. I continued, in spite of pain, in spite of lung inflammation, ribcage tension, and liver damage. I continued, no matter what anyone said. I had faith, and I persisted in hope. I'm too pragmatic to accept that age forty two is the end of hope. I learned to have a dogged sense of determination. I learned to see any progress as a 'win', and learned to stop to celebrate even the smallest victory. Walking up stairs without being out of breath. Carrying groceries without upper back spasms afterwards. Driving for more than an hour without my spine seizing up. Being able to be in a city for an hour, with a nebuliser. Tiny steps of progress led to more tiny steps, led to larger steps. Here I am, six years later, walking, doing proper cardio again, most of the inflammation under control, my lungs being largely settled for the first time in years. Don't ever lose hope. And ignore anybody who says you should.

Love

Love isn't about being seen, being heard, having a reputation. It's a quiet, still, internal thing. It's about believing in others, seeing them and their capacities, offering support, kindness, and loyalty. It's not about 'views', or 'likes', or 'sales'. It means doing something for the pure joy of it, trusting that the act alone has meaning. Love in business? It's about valuing people, valuing ourselves, valuing humanity. It's about being willing to go the extra mile, not for the sale, but simply because someone will benefit. For Gadfly, it's about designing transformational experiences, with love.

We can have faith that the work we do will make a difference. We can hope that it touches many peoples' lives. Without love, that intangible thing, that desire to truly make a difference, to see lives changed, to see people flourish and thrive, as a result of contact, all of the rest is meaningless. Organisational or personal change can only make a meaningful difference if it is deeply personal, deeply heartfelt, deeply human, deeply loving. Sure, without love, the 'numbers' may be a bit better. Engagement scores may increase. Employee 'satisfaction' may improve, but you and I both know that's not the same as an organisation that feels and shows genuine, heartfelt care. That's why love is the future of business: it's the only way out of this mess.

> *We can change our view of ourselves,*
> *simply by explaining our perspective.*

I left the church because I didn't want to be pressured into preaching about things I didn't believe. And here I am, years later, starting a spiritual revolution, and I'm even using biblical words to make my point. The triad of faith, hope, and love has its origins in a letter, sent a few thousand years ago by the Apostle Paul, to the church in Corinth, Greece. It's amazing how, by looking back, remembering and accepting our past, we can look to our future with hope.

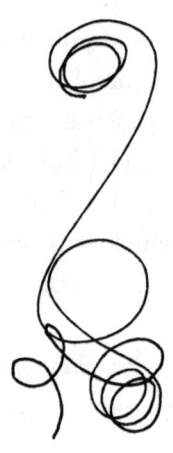

Postlude

I'm sitting at the top of *Campo Dei Fiori*, at the old military helipad. There's a 360 degree panorama from here, with views over Como to the east, the Prealps to the north, *Lago Maggiore* and *Monte Rosa* to the west, and the Milanese plain to the south. The sun is setting over the Alps, and lighting the brown layer of pollution that hangs in the air over the whole area. Just below me is the tree where I saw baby owls last year. Dante is pulling on the leash, wanting to run. I'm mulling the journey I've been on while writing this book, and how to somehow tie it all together. I'm not sure I can really tie it all together, though, or why I should. It's a mixed assortment of personal stories, metaphor, journeys, snippets of experiences with clients, models for working with organisations and individuals, personal reflections, art. It's your meanings, your reflections, your projections, your responses that will tie it all together for you.

Dante just interrupted my writing with hunting yelps, and I need to hold him. I need to be the one who decides when we hunt, or he will think he's in charge, and my life

Postlude

will become a hellish series of yelps. One second.

I'm tempted to leave everything open and loose, hanging in mid-air, and leave it for you to deal with. It maybe seems unfair, or like I'm making you do the work. I need to think through this a little more carefully. The boundary between what is my work, and what is your work, is really important. I can't make everything neat and tidy for you. I can't reduce the complexity. I can't make it simpler, or more complex, than it is.

The clouds are lit up with the last rays of the sun. I'll take a photo, and see if it works to add it to the book. The colours are amazing. I'm sad that you won't be able to see them, as the book is only printed in black and white. The air smells of leaves, mushrooms, and autumn. The moon is rising, and is almost full. In the distance, I can see planes landing at Milan's three airports, but here, up on the mountain, the sound of crickets is louder. That, and Dante, who is now whining to himself. It's strange, looking at the second peak and seeing the book cover. It's been an incredible journey of discovery for me, and one that I'm going to have a hard time setting down. Maybe that's why I don't want to neatly tie everything together. I don't want this experience to end.

I just got to the wild part of the walk, where we head into the woods. Dante sits, waiting for me to let him off the leash. Before I had time to say 'go', he has rushed into the woods, and is bounding across the forest floor, hunting for boar, deer, anything that he can chase. So far, thankfully, he's found nothing.

Writing this book has changed me. It has reminded me of parts of myself I had forgotten, because they were inconvenient, too difficult to fit into a 'normal' life, or a 'normal' business book. Walking in the wilds again, allowing myself to explore and reconnect with the joy of uncharted territory, have awoken parts of me that were dormant, neglected. I've been walking on this mountain for over eight hundred days in a row, give or take a few. I'm not tired of it. Wow. The sky has turned volcano red, over the whole chain of Alps. It's breathtaking.

Even though I've walked here so much, there was a wilder part of me, an older part of me that I was leaving aside. Too wild. Too energetic. Too lively. I can hear my teachers now, my bosses, my supervisors, clients, co-workers. But there's nothing wrong with wanting to run in the forest, howling. Just because other people don't want to do it, doesn't mean it's wrong.

I didn't ever set out to change anything. I only ever wanted to be *me*. I made the mistake, over almost forty years of my life, of looking *outside* myself for that permission. Waiting for a place that would be ok with it, an environment in which I would be given permission. But right here, all along, the permission was waiting. Right outside my door. The wilds, the woods, the mountains. Places that I forgot I belonged. Places that are my home. I'm strangely grateful for the mould, the damp, and the asthma, for the nights of coughing, the agony of not being able to breathe. They drove me to the mountains, on the suggestion of my pulmonologist. Without suffering, I wouldn't have rediscovered the depth to which it's possible to feel alive. So now I have a new target: to get fit enough that I can eventually run in the mountains again like in my twenties, hopping from rock

Postlude

to rock, learning from the mountain goats and chamoix. If only I could find a way to use my wildness in my work. Perhaps that's my next big challenge; integrating what I've learned through this experience. It's ok, really ok, I mean absolutely, completely, and totally fine for me to be myself in my work, no matter what other people think. Thinking back ten years, to conversations I had with my then coach, Ron Mills, about the book I wanted to write on creativity in business, I would have told you that I was 100% comfortable being myself in my work. But I was hiding a lot of things from myself, so I could avoid the pain of living a life that really wasn't mine. Corporations have a way of doing that to people. I've worked with hundreds of leaders who had a sense that there was something missing. I thought I had the answers. It turns out that I didn't.

Here's to your future of exploring, creating, wildness and wholeness. Here's to bringing 'crazy', bringing love, into the workplace. It turns out that it's not really that crazy after all. It's actually the world that has gone crazy, and has forgotten what it means to be human.

It's dark now. I need to pay attention to where I'm walking, so I can get to the car and head home. Thank you for joining me on this journey of discovery. I hope it's been useful to you, and I hope it continues far beyond the reading of this book. If you would like me to join you, your team, your organisation on your own journeys, please let me know. I would be honoured. The owl just hooted, and the moon is bright. Time to go. Please keep safe. And please keep exploring; it's how you'll find the love in life, and in business.

*Nothing really ends: it just gets recycled,
repurposed, reinvented.*

I know, the book is finished, but the process of creating it hasn't. I want to keep you in the process until the end. Today, I'm driving up into the mountains again, to *Valle Verzasca*, an amazing valley in Switzerland with giant pools in the river that are swimmable. I've not been here since 1996, the year before I moved to America to start the PhD that I didn't ever complete. I'm such a different person, yet fundamentally the same. It's amazing to feel the differences and the similarities, as I head on this trip. 23 years ago, I came here in a group, on a Sunday afternoon after church. I didn't feel that it was right to go swimming on a Sunday. My parents would find out, and they would criticise me, sharing the story with others of how 'unholy' I had been on a Sunday. I told people that I didn't feel well, and sat watching them splashing and diving in the deep blue water.

It's the second Thursday in September. It's far too cold for Swiss or Italians to go wild swimming; only 19 degrees; time for sweaters, after the long, warm summer. When I started writing, the daytime temperature was 33 degrees, and the coldest it got was 22. In two weeks, the temperature has dropped by ten degrees, and I'm finding myself shivering any time I'm not wearing long sleeves. The water will be freezing, as the first snow came last weekend. I have my back-pack, passport, swimming shorts, and a printed copy of a 240-page book that only two weeks ago was a collection of ideas. I wrote the postlude last night, and decided to read the whole thing today, to see if there

Postlude

are any gaps, areas that need to be changed, edited, or cut out. I now have six hours in which to read, scribble notes, and swim in the river. I'm tempted to look up the 'best location in Verzasca for wild swimming', but I don't want to. I want to explore a bit, trust my instincts, and see where that leads me. It's becoming a habit after doing it for two weeks solid.

Driving up the valley, past the giant dam, there are large billboard posters, in French, German, and Italian, warning of the dangers of swimming. Photos of toddlers jumping in, men slipping on rocks, with emotionally intrusive straplines like "just one moment of inattention", "it takes nothing to slip", "post on social media before you swim, so people know where you are". Swiss risk management seems a bit paranoid here. But tourists haven't been schooled in the ways of the wild, and I'm sure more and more people have been injured here, as it's popularity has increased thanks to Instagram.

What I remember as a wild, lost valley now has paid parking along its length, tourist signs, and on every rock, there's a 20-something taking a selfie. But the warnings seem to have worked. Nobody is swimming. The idyll is now like some sort of amusement park. I head to the end of the valley. The villages are littered with "family hotel", "bed and breakfast" and "traditional restaurant" signs, all in English. The truly traditional eating places in this area don't have signs, and don't even speak Italian. They speak *Ticinese* dialect, and wouldn't be interested in serving foreigners. I can't reach the end of the valley. It is reserved for permit holders, so I'm funnelled into a paid car park. I'm torn. Do I persist, and try to find some wild here, or do I give up? I've driven thirty minutes further than planned, and all I'm seeing is more and more ways that whoever owns the valley can make money. Thirty three years ago, when I was first in this valley on a school trip, it was in decline. The farm outbuildings that are now 'traditional restaurants' were collapsing, and the local villagers invited schools to help with rebuilding their heritage. We had lessons on the architecture, the way of life, the history.

Verzasca has completed the transition from being an ancient valley in decline, to a contemporary, trade marked, commercialised, tourist trap. The farmers now use strimmers instead of scythes, and the valley resonates with them. I don't want this 'branded' experience. I want the wilderness that I knew from twenty years ago. As I stand, looking at the parking payment options, ten Swiss francs for the day, another bus load of tourists unloads, filling the village at the end of the valley with French, German, and English. I get in my car to leave. I don't think nature should be privatised. I read more about the parking here. The local commune decided to put it in place as tourism was increasing to a level that the local village couldn't afford to pay for maintaining the damage to paths and removal of rubbish left by visitors. The regional director of tourism: "nature doesn't clean itself". Maybe the 10 francs should include a lesson about responsibility in nature.

When we don't accept imperfection,
we reject ourselves. That serves nobody.

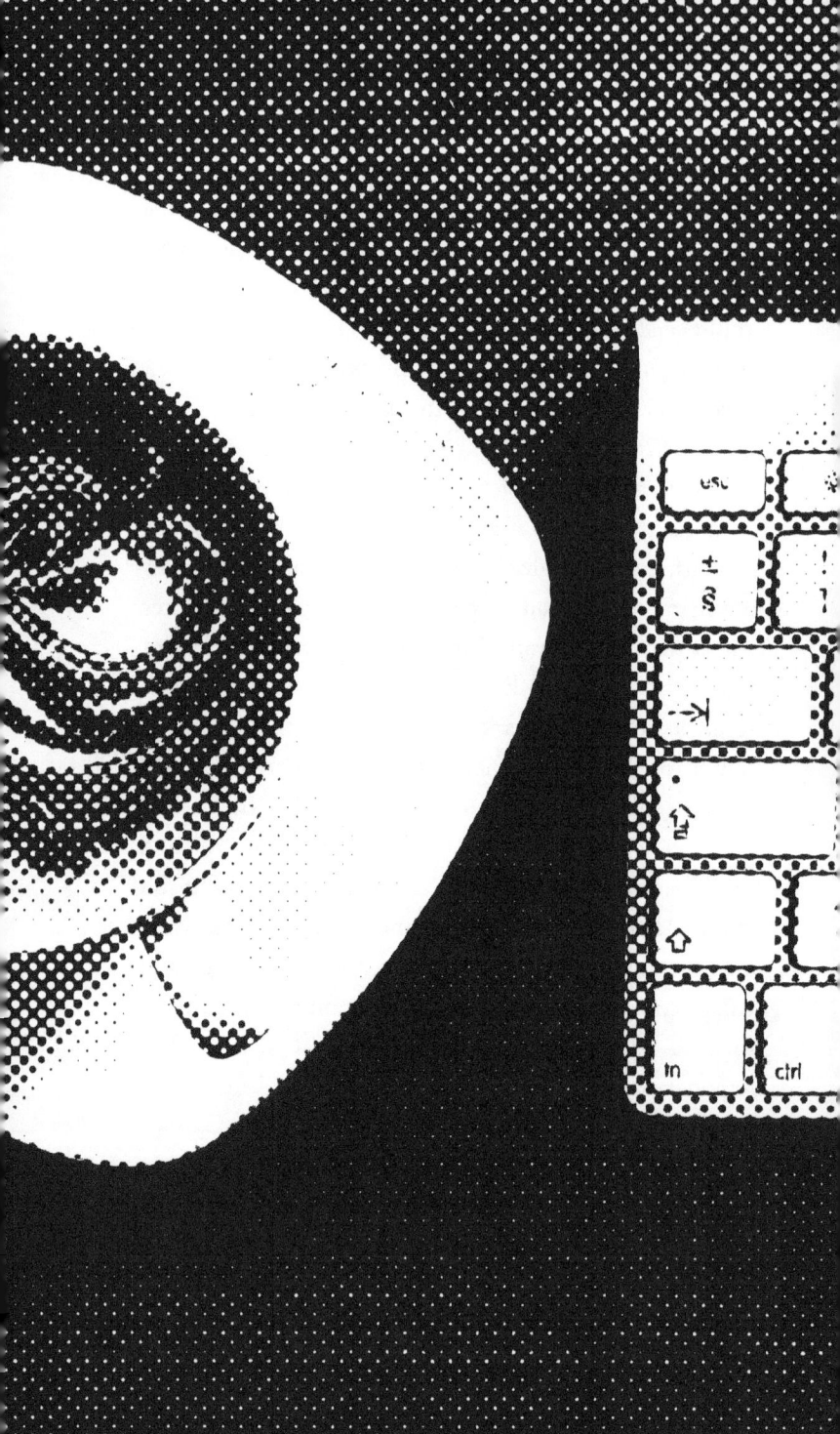

Day 15. I am eating the last of the blueberry jam, with yoghurt and a cappuccino, while editing. I'm on page fifty seven, reading about Georges, and I'm crying. The journey of the last two weeks has been extraordinary. I didn't ever think that writing a book could change me this much, and reveal so many things I had forgotten about myself. I'm also sad that the jam is gone. I am determined to build a new Gadfly business, as me. With my wild bits, my swanky bits, my expensive-suit-loving bits, and my wild mountain boy bits, all woven together like the parts of this book. It's messy, contradictory, imperfect, and human. Like I am. Like we all are.

We are the future of business. And as humans, one of our greatest capacities is to accept and value our imperfection, our messiness, our contrariness: to love. Imagine how enormous the impact could be if we all showed more love towards ourselves, our colleagues, clients, providers, bosses, investors, and environment.

It's almost 2am now. It's been a long day. Dante is slumped on his bed, waiting for me. He won't go to sleep until I do, and he's really bored of this editing. Wolf hierarchy etiquette is strange. It's taken a sixteen hour day of editing to get to the end of the book. The hardest part was the emotional intensity of some sections, with their ferocious hairpin turns, and nausea inducing humps. I knew that this book would be special, but I didn't expect this. Ferocious clarity, sharpness, humanity, and only a few parts that don't quite feel right. It's been an overwhelming experience reading through it all at once. Some parts I couldn't be more pleased with.

Postlude

Some felt so dense that I will have to take another look tomorrow. I'm happy with the shape of it, and the edits that I've made on paper today should tighten the flow. A few more tweaks, and it will be done.

I'm almost too tired to type on my phone. My eyes are closing. It's time for bed. I have a manuscript of 247 printed pages filled with scribbled analogue comments. It's been a long fifteen and a half days. The remaining tweaks are likely to take another few weeks before proofreading, detailed feedback, and marketing. It's almost surreal to think back to the first day, to remember my fear that I wouldn't finish it in time to submit it for distribution in mid November, as planned, so we can hit a January publication date. I don't even know how I feel. I'm that tired. The one thing I do know is that I'm looking forward to having this final phase over with, so you and I can have a conversation over a coffee, leaving the book sitting on the table.

What if our lives are metaphors? Things to learn from, share, reflect on, and tell stories about?

I have an editing hangover. My brain is sluggish, as I transfer the edits into the final manuscript. I've started a to-do list, while drinking a cappuccino: spell-check, audit for over-zealous italics, homogenise use of quotation marks, fix a few sections. I won't tell you which, in case you look too closely at them, and see the joins and patching. You probably noticed them anyway. I don't want to keep writing. I think that the useful commentary on the process is done, and another ten pages of detail about file conversions, uploads, proofing won't be useful to anybody. This isn't a book about how to make a book. I added the commentary on my creative process to remove some of the mystery, some of the distance, the podium that writers hide behind. I wanted to use the process of writing as a metaphor for transformation, change, flow, and growth. Writing and organisational change are both fundamentally about relationship.

> *Life is more simple than we think it is:*
> *that's its complexity.*

A week later, the design is finalised. The text has been checked and re-checked. The typesetting is finished. The artwork is inserted. The first version has been sent to proofreaders. I'm sitting with a completed book, and I'm feeling overwhelmed. I've been texting with Villy, my trusty detail designer, and Mary, my editor, about the final choices for the cover. We're trying to decide whether love should be capitalised or not, upper case or not. We've all changed our minds at least three or four times, and spent about an hour on the decision. Upper case feels so serious, so heavy, so formal. Lower case feels too fluffy. Capitalised just feels right. Love is imperfect, slightly imbalanced, a bit uneven. It's *human*.

I print the cover designs, and ask Tristan what he thinks. He immediately says "I like the combination of capitals and not. It's more balanced. The capitals seem like they're shouting at me, and the lower case is too wooly." No hesitation. The simple wisdom of an almost 15 year old.

Postlude

This is the final page. As I write, I'm very aware that I don't want 'this' to end. But this is my work, and our work. This is the work we all have to do, to ensure that the future is more human. I want this book to be a beginning, a starting point, a new chapter for everyone who reads it. I want to start a movement. I want Gadfly, while it exists, to be an organisation that moves the world, emotionally, spiritually, and existentially. I want us all to remember what really matters in life—beyond money, beyond consumption, beyond profit.

Acknowledgements

I would like to thank all of my clients and collaborators from the last seventeen years of work in creativity, leadership and organisational development. I have grown alongside you, and many of our conversations are woven throughout this book. I wish I could thank you all personally.

BP, Johnson & Johnson, Lloyds Banking Group, HSBC, RBS Group, Toshiba, Sodexo, Steinway, Jones Lang Lasalle, Zurich Insurance Group, Barclays, EFG Private Bank, Nomura International, Aviva, Lombard, GMT Partners, TPG Capital, Nova Capital, Standard Bank, Natwest, Santander International, Coutts, Barclays Capital, ABN Amro, Direct Line Group, Metro Bank, Standard Life, Tesco Bank, RBS International, Northern Rock, Ernst & Young, The BBC, BAE Systems, PWC, Royal Bank of Scotland, Ethicon, Carillion, Compass Group, Sheppard Moscow, UGL, DTZ, Cushman & Wakefield, Turner and Townsend, CBRE, Sodexo, Procurian, Accenture, Johnson Controls, University of Strathclyde, Edinburgh International Festival, Scottish Opera, Tangible, Channings, 2gether Partnership, Creative Realities, Center for Creative Leadership, Cantle, Snook, Fuchsia Blue, Caret, Harvard University, Comotion, YSC, Change Management International, Nile, Bunnyfoot, Metro Bank, IMG Artists, Innotown, Creative Leaps International, Victoria & Albert, Fazioli, Citigroup, Acorn Principle Plus, Edinburgh Festival

Theatre, North Edinburgh Arts, We Create, Pallacanestro Varese, Downie Allison Downie, 999 design, Creative Scotland, Arts & Business, Glasgow School of Art, Really Useful Group, Michael Clark Company, The Movement Studio, Dance House, Metropolis Studios, Sylph Editions, Fenner Paper, Ingram.

There are particular individuals I would like to thank, without whose influence this book wouldn't exist. Georges Affolter, for showing me the value of love. Mary McDonough, for tolerating nineteen days of me in deep creative process, for editing, proof-reading, advising, supporting, and being patient with me. Nastia Tyagar, for just being herself, and reminding me to climb trees. Brendan and Tristan, for being teenagers, and keeping me humble, stressed, and aware of all of my imperfections on a daily basis. Dante, for reminding me of the importance of being wild, and for skipping a few walks so that I could complete this project. Villy Tentoma Zervou for showing me that the simple things matter, and for lending her amazing eye for detail. Giulia Berardi, for inspiring me to finally create this book. Richard Merrick, for his patience, support, and 'Boomer' insights. Frank Laine, who taught me to not to take anything I see at face value. Ron Mills, without whose coaching this book wouldn't have got started. Jeremy Cull, for sharing music with me. David Horth, for long conversations about creativity. Malcolm Fortune, for his example of how to run a personal business. Sophie Bancroft, for introducing me to jazz, and being patient with my process. Ian Harrison, for his friendship and coaching that reminded me that being spiritual matters.

Diarmid Baillie and Carolyn Dougill, for their loving presence in my life at a time when I needed it. Laurent Haquin, for giving me a grounding in martial arts. Zio Zak, for showing me that there are very different paths in life. Dr Peter Kewin, Donald Sinclair, and other medical professionals who helped me on the path to recovery. Michelle Armstrong, Jim McNeish, and Anne Lonsdale, for welcoming me on their coaching programmes when I needed to find my way in life. Edinburgh Coaching Hub, for the opportunity to learn from leading, and for the creative stimulus. John Wilson, for deep conversations about ethics, responsibility and spirituality, and robust challenges. Connie Johnson, for her imperfect but valuable love.

Thanks to Sheryl Phillips, Ailsa Suttie, Helena Clayton, Pauline Lindsay, Paul Nayar, and Gavin Peacock for reading, and Stephen Aris, Martin Knox and Philip Soanes for reminding me that empathy really matters.

Thanks to Richard O'Connor, Sezgin Kaya, Daniele at Blackblade, Alessio De Marco, Alice Matteucci, Remo and Lucia from Trattoria Pizzeria Tramonti, Clive Broome from the Bluebell Railway, Zoe McColl, Rachel Rose Reid, Marc McColgan, David Ide, Keith Williams, Mr Quaintance, Keel Watson, Pavel Golenistsev, Oliver Lee, Matteo Bianchi, Jean-Marc Charpilloz, and Stéphanie Coudray, for their parts in my story.

I'm really grateful to the Gadfly interns who last year helped to kick-start my writing and creating for this book, when I was too ill to think very clearly: Josie Do Nizza, Mohammed Kobari, Shoheil Bhowmick, Taban Astaraki, Varia Erikhova, Ana-Maria Manole.

Index

A
achieving 29
affection 148
aggressive 58, 59
Ailsa 214
alignment 187
alive 70, 71, 73, 90, 118, 119, 120, 127, 136, 201
Alps 46, 144, 199, 201
analysis 13, 45, 128, 130, 191
anti-consumerist 111
apologise 14, 27, 29, 41, 42, 43, 44, 80, 130
apologising 41, 45
Aretha 88
art 78, 117, 125, 130, 155, 157, 165, 192, 199
art galleries 192
Articles 139, 142
artist 153, 155, 159
artwork 209
asthma 20, 22, 92, 95, 195, 201
attraction 174
authentic 125, 166, 172
authentically 57, 151
automation 57, 67
avoidance 172, 174, 175, 176
awe-inspiring 30, 32, 66, 80, 127

B
barber 55, 56
basketball 73, 74, 75
battery chicken 155
battery hens 154
beauty 32, 165
behaviours 60, 87, 135, 166, 178, 183
beliefs 41, 46, 79, 89, 111, 124, 133, 166, 171, 175, 180, 194
belief systems 78
Bentley 141
berries 99
beyond 20, 24, 28, 136
biblical 197
blind spots 42
Bluebell Railway 143, 144
blueberries 47, 95, 98, 99, 100, 108, 119, 121, 191
blueberry 207
blueprint 69, 80
blueprints 69
boar 22, 40, 58, 200
board meeting 140
boardroom 87, 113, 155, 191
boardrooms 142
boards 142
bodies 156
Boomer 42, 44, 213
border 19, 31, 34
boredom 136, 175
Bösendorfer 150
boxes 15, 36, 37
branding 30, 56, 116, 166, 173
Brendan 24, 33, 34, 43, 74, 213

businesses 50, 52, 57, 112, 114, 130, 183, 185

C

Campo Dei Fiori 39, 58, 71, 199
capitalist 111
care 83
certainty 129
chairmen 142
change 22, 30, 34, 52
  at scale 15
  essence of 36
  large scale 20
  leaders 42
  organisational 13, 50
  organisational change 209
  power to 50
  programmes 183
  systemic 50
childhood 47
choices 25
Christian 46, 157, 181
church 19, 46, 88, 140, 142, 155, 156, 158, 181, 197, 203
clarity 37
clouds 200
coaching 13, 20, 27, 51, 74, 124, 149, 158, 166, 169, 173, 178, 213, 214
collaboration 161, 183
comfortable 27, 29
companies 57, 64, 66, 75, 96, 111, 114, 119, 125, 142, 148, 158, 182, 191
compassion 86, 127
Concorde 16, 141, 142
confidentiality 168
confusion 175
congruence 185
consultancy 13, 20, 39, 66
consumer 25, 52

consumerism 66
consumerist 30, 64
consumption 52, 67, 132, 210
contemplation 119
contradictory 37
contrariness 207
conventional 13, 38, 46, 128
conversational 171
core condition 142
  core conditions 67, 140, 161, 169
Corinth 197
corporate 13, 57
corporation 39, 51, 52, 66, 69, 76, 80, 103, 104, 108, 114, 115, 142, 180, 194
Corporations 93
counter-cultural 78
countries 31, 51
cover 209
cows 19, 33
crafting 165, 193
crazy 20, 40, 42, 43, 53
  slightly crazy 134
creativity 13, 30, 39, 51, 115, 116, 136, 191, 202, 212
  creating 39, 42, 45
criticising 45, 59
cultural 77
cultural conditioning 79
cultural norms 78
culture 68, 77, 87, 88, 96, 98, 129, 134, 177, 182
  company culture 139
  counter-cultural 79
  cultures 140

D

dance 109, 159
dancing 16, 156, 159
Dante 22, 58, 59, 60, 73, 88, 95, 98, 199, 207, 213
Debussy 151

decisions 32, 60
deep 24, 38, 45, 48, 52, 53, 129
deer 22, 37, 38, 40, 58, 200
defences 42
defunct 29
denial 59, 132
design 4, 31, 35, 36, 117, 164, 165, 180, 181, 184, 186, 192
  experience 165, 180, 192, 193
designer 36
destination 34, 127
destruction 70, 118, 136, 146, 194
dialogue 97, 98, 104, 105, 114, 124, 129, 130, 191
direction 15, 19, 29, 43, 50
draft 32, 35

E

economies 68
editing 4, 36, 165, 179, 193, 207, 208, 213
editor 27, 32, 36
effectiveness 39
efficiency 25, 28, 31, 40, 60, 67, 128, 132, 182
effort 128, 136
ego 42
emerge 36
engaging 27, 136
environment 31, 32, 39, 40, 52
ephemeral 125, 186
era 51, 127
essence 24, 36, 57
ethical 85, 87, 88
everyday 127, 157
executive coaching 13, 27
  executive coaches 42
executives 13
existential 96, 105, 117, 123, 125, 127, 132, 136, 186
experiment 69
exploration 28, 31, 42, 103, 163, 164, 171, 175, 185, 191
explore 78
explorer 24

F

faith 46, 148, 194, 195, 196, 197
famine 194
fast food 62, 64
fasting 92
fear 44, 66, 92, 96, 98, 132, 147, 148, 155, 181, 208
  fear-based 97, 182
  fears 41
feedback 27, 41, 79, 104, 121, 123, 124, 170, 208
financial stress 81, 82
fingers 99, 100, 101, 160, 166
flooding 194
flow 34, 39, 50
flowing 25
font size 164
forests 19, 27, 31, 46
formatting 32
frames of reference 20, 166
francs 33, 205
friends 55, 134
frustration 25, 27
future corporations 69

G

Gadfly principles 37, 123, 178, 179
generations 19, 24, 48
genuine 27, 57, 129, 130, 136
Georges 7, 46, 47, 48, 50, 94, 118, 150, 207
Giulia 65, 213

Glasgow 147, 148, 213
global 66
globalisation 64
global warming 194
goal 28, 29, 30, 136
Granny 154
gratitude 48
growth 52, 67, 68, 109, 111, 112, 113, 115, 135, 136, 140, 161, 181, 183, 184, 185, 209

H

habits 94, 168, 184
harmony 52
Heisenberg 181
Helena 189, 214
hens 153, 154
hierarchy 59, 60, 106, 109, 114, 182, 207
honesty 82, 183
honing 165, 184
honour 42
horizons 127
hugs 131, 147, 148
  free hugs 147
  hugging 136, 148
human 22, 37, 39, 40, 52, 58, 60, 80, 133, 135, 137
  being 42, 46, 133, 136
  business 179
  corporation 66
  societies 60
  spirit 39
  system 59
  touch 57
humanity 60, 70, 80, 105, 109, 115, 148, 197, 207

I

illness 133
imagination 33
impact 32, 60

imperfect 116, 117, 124, 133, 191, 207, 214
improvisation 191
  improvisational 187
  improvise 45
inconsistency 37
incorporating 32
individuals 84, 97, 119, 127, 147, 172, 177, 185, 199, 213
industrial 31, 57, 60, 136
inequality 194
inflammation 93, 94, 95, 196
inspiration 34
instinct 38, 48, 128
integration 32
intent 28, 32, 41, 42, 165
irritation 14, 27, 37
  irritated 33, 40, 41, 42
Italy 20, 22, 32, 34, 55, 60, 64, 65, 74, 75, 87, 91, 157, 177
iteration 187
  iterative 187

J

jacket 146, 165
jam 47, 52, 94, 99, 108, 118, 121, 150, 191, 207
Jam is Life 47, 192
jazz 159, 213
jigsaw 178
joy 30, 47
judgement 45

K

kindness 86, 106, 130, 196

L

landscape
  psychological 85, 178
laughing 43
leaders 13, 20, 42, 77, 78, 112, 114, 135, 146, 149, 161, 168, 182, 192, 202

leadership 13, 20, 77, 83, 107, 112, 114, 120, 212
life 38, 40, 47, 48, 68, 82, 89, 90, 96, 100, 117, 127, 128, 129, 131, 135, 145, 146, 147
  being alive 127
  jam 47, 52
  philosophy 47
  skill 128
  whole 20, 52
limit 28, 34, 63, 64, 65
linear 32, 135
listen 86, 130, 153, 170
listening 56, 94, 105, 149, 156, 159, 164, 168, 170, 182
liver 92, 93, 195, 196
local 66
logical 32
love 22, 24, 32, 34, 39, 47, 48, 53, 56, 58, 64, 130, 132, 161, 173, 186, 196, 207
  building business with 27
  definition of 30
  loving 32, 52
  self-love 161
  the future of business 186
loving 32, 52, 127, 157, 197, 207, 213

M

magical 33, 37, 43
management 31
manuscript 36, 208
map 174
margins 67, 164
marketing 80, 208
marmots 44
martial art 130
Mary 15, 21, 31, 32, 37, 38, 43, 81, 95, 103, 104, 108, 121, 164, 209, 213
Master 106, 107, 146
meandering 27, 28, 44, 80, 105, 175, 176, 191
meaning 32, 70, 76, 89, 90, 119, 123, 127, 133, 136, 151, 161, 187, 191, 196
measurement 183
meditation 123, 159
meditative 130
Mediterranean 119, 121
metaphor 209
metaphors 27, 44
milk 47, 139
millimetre 163
minimalist 31
model 29, 57
models 29, 68, 69, 135, 166, 181, 182, 199
Monte Rosa 199
motivation 21, 48, 149
motorway 33, 53, 63
movement 159, 180, 210
mushrooms 20, 24, 28, 29, 33, 47
music 13, 56, 88, 90, 119, 125, 145, 150, 156, 157, 158, 159, 213

N

narcissism 135
narrative 15, 37
natural 20, 22, 25, 31, 47, 52, 53, 56, 58, 59
nature 22, 24, 30, 31, 32, 34, 37, 40, 46, 47, 48, 50, 53, 132
  deer 22, 37, 38, 40, 58
  forests 19, 27, 31, 46
  marmots 44
  mountains 19, 20, 22, 23, 29, 31, 35, 38, 41, 46, 47, 53, 131

natural order 52, 58
respect for nature 30, 32
river 34, 46, 50
stream 35, 37, 40, 42, 43, 48, 50, 53
trees 38, 47
valley 37, 38, 43, 46, 47, 48
wild 19, 20, 22, 23, 24, 31, 32, 33, 35, 40, 43, 53, 58, 59, 60, 132
nebuliser 196
notes 13, 28, 124, 169, 171, 204

O

Opera 157, 158, 159, 212
operating system 184
organisation 28, 39, 52, 69, 75, 87, 114, 129, 140, 142, 149, 161, 166, 170, 172, 182, 197, 202, 210
organisational 13, 50, 66, 166, 170, 173, 209, 212
organisations 14, 28, 32, 39, 60, 69, 76, 79, 89, 114, 115, 116, 123, 134, 136, 148, 155, 161, 172, 183, 192, 199
outcome 69, 77, 130, 135, 165, 175
outcomes 79, 81, 106, 107, 125, 127, 166, 172, 193

P

page
  pages 35, 70, 160, 163, 164, 165, 175, 208, 209
  turning 164
paper 70, 71, 140, 143, 163, 164, 208
paperback 164
paradox 31, 77, 90, 129
  paradoxical 37
paradoxical 37, 79, 125, 179, 186
paradoxical positions 179
paragraphs 15, 37, 179, 181, 184
parents 141, 143, 148, 150, 156, 157, 203
passion 58, 74, 75, 76, 90, 124, 136, 146, 150, 176, 177
passions 56, 57
patience 27, 128, 130
patterns 171, 172
Pavel 66
peace 31, 33, 34, 35, 53
peaceful 34, 48
peak 67
perfection 91, 117, 118, 136, 166
performance 124, 157, 158
performer 84, 155, 156
performing 84, 86, 145, 155, 156, 157, 158
permission 4, 37, 60, 148, 155, 201
personal stories 13, 14
perspective 15, 51, 123, 129, 131, 133
  perspectives 77, 104, 124, 128, 130
perspectives 77, 104, 124, 128, 130
pheasant 153
philosophical 39, 51, 60, 68, 107, 115, 123, 125, 179, 181
philosophy 13, 14, 31, 39, 40, 42, 47, 50, 52, 66, 80, 106, 108, 114, 124, 137, 169, 183, 186
  design philosophy 31
phone 43, 50, 100, 208
physical 30, 67, 68, 70
physics 13, 68, 166

Physics 20, 67, 116, 157, 181
physiotherapist 195
pianist 150
piano 88, 91, 119, 150, 151, 153, 154, 155, 159
plan 25, 29, 31, 34, 35
  planning 25, 29, 31, 34, 35
planet 32, 132
play 75, 76, 105, 150, 151, 186
  permission to 155
pondering 34, 50
power 20, 32, 47, 50
present 31, 40, 57, 78, 127, 160, 161, 174, 176, 185, 186
presentation 166
principles 13, 37, 67, 78, 124, 172, 178, 179, 181, 193
problem 13, 40
products 57, 76, 80, 84, 95, 117, 119, 120, 125, 136, 177
profit 39, 51, 60, 64, 65, 66, 67, 69, 94, 164, 210
profound 34
progress 100, 101
project 38, 88, 115, 171, 213
proofreaders 209
proofreading 208
prototype 69, 80
psychological splits 179
psychologist 66
psychology 52, 69, 85, 86, 94, 166
psychotherapy 13, 27, 166, 169
  therapy 14, 45
pulmonologist 21, 201
punishment 160
purpose 28, 51, 65, 89, 108, 125, 127, 177, 191
puzzle 15

Q

questioning 79
questions 127, 183

R

Rachmaninov 150
reader 14, 25, 27, 41, 42, 44, 103
real 56, 57, 136
reality 58, 68, 70, 77, 132
received wisdom 24
recording studios 192
reframing 78
refugees 120
relationship 37, 42, 53, 78, 83, 111, 115, 116, 130, 151, 161, 168, 173, 177, 182, 186, 209
respect 20, 30, 32, 59, 132
revenue 75
rhythm 25, 159
Richard 41, 42, 43, 44, 45, 51, 76, 104, 106, 124, 175, 213
Rieti 61, 65, 66
risk management 96, 180, 204
river 34, 46, 50, 107, 119, 156, 203, 204
Rolls Royce 141
rules 45, 79, 108, 114, 124, 147, 148, 168, 177, 179, 183
running 15, 23, 24, 61, 67, 68, 76, 78, 109, 111, 118, 128, 142, 144

S

safety 24, 60, 144, 168, 169, 176
sales 39, 75, 84, 85, 86, 87, 183, 196
section 37, 39, 41, 44
September 91, 98, 99, 203
serious 20, 95, 141, 142

services 136
shareholders 93
silence 33, 34, 56
simple 47, 48, 50
sinful 156
sit 33, 34, 35
sketch 172
sketches 184
ski 99, 146, 147, 150
skiing 144
skill 128
Slave 106, 107, 146
social collapse 194
social media 56
social structure 58
society
  industrial societies 136
  modern society 128
sociopathy 87
soft 14, 130
speeding ticket 63
spiritual 13, 32, 39, 51, 52, 69, 76, 92, 98, 109, 114, 115, 135, 136, 142, 194, 197, 213
  corporation 39, 51, 52
  growth 135
  spirituality 30
spiritual sustainability 142
sponsorship 75
spring 31, 35, 50, 53, 132
stagnant 182
Steinway 151
stream 35, 37, 40, 42, 43, 48, 50, 53
suffering 48, 67, 128, 132, 180, 201
Sunday 157, 203
sunshine 33
superficial 127, 183
supermarkets 93
surgery 19, 20, 32
sustainability 142
sustainable 120
swim 66, 204
Switzerland 19, 22, 23, 31, 32, 34, 38, 46, 47, 95, 98, 103, 143, 146, 150, 177, 203
system change 50
systems analysis 13

T

terms of engagement 168
territory 25, 29, 58, 60
testing 24, 28, 34, 36
thickness 163, 165
threads 42, 44
touching 148
track 19, 28, 32, 33, 44, 46
traditional 55, 76, 204, 205
train 143, 144, 146
trains 143, 144
transformation 120, 166, 173, 193, 209
transformational 166, 193, 194, 197
tribal 89
Tristan 42, 209, 213
trust 32, 42, 129, 136
truth 42, 52, 129
turnaround 13, 120, 161
typesetting 209

U

uncomfortable 86, 164
universe 52, 132
unknown 20, 77, 78, 79, 81
urges 51
useful 27, 44, 128, 131, 136

V

value beyond money 70
values 57, 106, 108, 116, 146, 161, 169, 171, 174

anti-values 174
core values 171
Verzasca 193, 203, 204, 205
Villy 120, 209, 213
Vipassana 123
vision 51, 66, 108, 116, 161, 165
voice 37, 124, 151, 158, 159
Voice of Leadership 77, 81, 97, 176
volcano 201

W

walk 19, 21, 23, 24, 25, 27, 28, 30, 33, 35, 43, 44, 47, 58
waste 70
wealth 47, 48, 136
We Are Basketball 65
what if 29, 37, 180
wild 22, 23, 24, 32, 33, 35, 40, 43, 53, 58, 59, 60, 132
wildness 20, 31, 191, 202
wisdom 24, 50, 52, 128
wolfdog 22, 59, 131
wolves 31
workplaces 29

Y

yoga 159
yoghurt 47, 108, 139, 140, 142, 150, 207

Z

Zen 14

GADFLY
www.gadflygroup.com

www.ingramcontent.com/pod-product-compliance
Lightning Source LLC
Chambersburg PA
CBHW020837160426
43192CB00007B/694